joy exhaustible.

ASSARACUS PRESENTS: THE PUBLISHERS
edited by Bryan Borland & Seth Pennington

SIBLING RIVALRY PRESS
ALEXANDER, ARKANSAS
WWW.SIBLINGRIVALRYPRESS.COM

EDITOR & PUBLISHER

Bryan Borland

EDITOR

Seth Pennington

Cover poem by Paul Mariah, "In Flight Over the Sierras: All Is Effort. Every Thing Is Full." Used by permission of his estate.

Sibling Rivalry Press
13913 Magnolia Glen Drive
Alexander, AR 72002
info@siblingrivalrypress.com

Printed in the United States of America.

ISBN: 978-1-937420-70-3
ISSN: 2159-0478
Library of Congress Control Number: 2014905002

Joy Exhaustible
Assaracus Presents: The Publishers
This anthology is simultaneously printed as *Assaracus*: Issue 14.
April 2014.

for JAMIE

&

for WULF

THE
PUBLISHERS

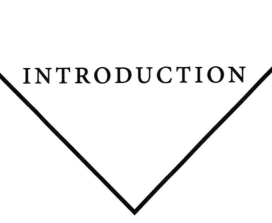

INTRODUCTION

THE PUBLISHERS

We, together, have arrived at *Assaracus* 14, which manifested in such a special way that we decided to publish it both as an issue of the journal for our subscribers and as a standalone anthology for purposes of longevity.

Assaracus was conceived as a space to allow gay poets to gather and showcase a significant body of work, a place where some of our more *queer* poems and certainly our *queer* poets, however one defines the word, could be published in one place. I said and repeated that I wanted to give gay poets a microphone; what they sang was up to them.

It's true that the first few issues were very lightly edited. I didn't see myself as an editor; with only one self-published book under my belt and a handful of publishing credits, I barely saw myself as a poet. Thus what you've witnessed, if you've been with me from the beginning, has been my education. I've certainly become a much stronger reader of poetry, which has informed my writing. And I think the poets who have appeared in our most recent issues would say that I've indeed become an editor. Each misspelling that escapes my eye leaves a scar, but know that the spirit in which I give you *Assaracus* echoes in Whitmanian tone:

> *POETS to come! orators, singers, musicians to come!*
> *Not to-day is to justify me, and answer what I am for;*
> *But you, a new brood, native, athletic, continental, greater than before known,*
> *Arouse! Arouse—for you must justify me—you must answer.*

And answer you have. Since our first issue, we've published nearly 150 self-identified gay poets (my favorite moment coming when we published the octogenarian Kirby Congdon alongside the teenage Peter LaBerge in Issue 11—and Kirby returns for this issue).

As *Assaracus* and my responsibility to curate and manage it has grown, along with those same duties as publisher (and tired-eyed proofreader, and PR person, and accountant, and secretary, and janitor) of Sibling Rivalry Press, I've found that my role as a writer has at times been eclipsed, if not in reality then in my own mind. When a poem is published or a positive or even a negative review of one of my own books appears, I enjoy the validation and the rush. With that in mind, I've decided to refocus on my own writing this year, but, as the gentlemen included in this issue will tell you, once a publisher, always a publisher. I can't separate my selves; thus what I've created is the Publisher's Issue of *Assaracus*, a space where the publishers and editors once again become the writers.

To turn this fantasy into a reality, I reached out to a group of publishers and editors—the contemporary and the history-making—and invited them to contribute. Note that those I invited were given the freedom to write in any style and on any subject, thus breaking the *gay poetry* rule of the journal. Together, these men have published some of the best of our gay poetry over the last fifty years, and they've earned the right to break that rule through long nights, frustration with printers, panic over typos, and service in roles as literary father figures to hundreds if not (collectively) thousands of writers.

I am indebted to the writers themselves—men who have been free with their advice to me when I've needed it, men generous in acts of kindness and promotion. They welcomed me into their club from the beginning. I'm also indebted to Philip Clark for helping me get in touch with the Paul Mariah estate, who graciously allowed his beautiful poem to appear on our cover. I thought it was fitting, particularly the line, "to revel in work is a joy exhaustible," from which we pulled the title. I also must thank my husband and fellow editor Seth Pennington, who reminds me every day why we do this, despite that joy exhaustible. He, like SRP, has changed my life completely. If you've been with me from the beginning, well, you know that story, too. And isn't that what *Assaracus* is all about? These are *our* stories.

Bryan Borland
March 8, 2014

FELICE PICANO

THE SEAHORSE PRESS

FELICE PICANO is the author of more than twenty-five books of poetry, stories, novels, memoirs, and non-fiction. His work has been translated into many languages. Several titles were national and international best sellers, and four of his plays have been produced, some often. He is considered a founder of modern gay literature along with the other members of the path-breaking Violet Quill Club. Picano was involved as writer or editor in early gay media such as *The Advocate*, *Out*, *Christopher Street*, and *The New York Native*. In 1977, Picano founded The SeaHorse Press, and then joined two friends in 1981 to form The Gay Presses of New York, which dominated the independent GLBT book scene for the next fifteen years. Picano's first novel was a finalist for the PEN/Hemingway Award in 1976. Since then he's been nominated for and/or won dozens of literary awards, including a Lambda Literary Foundation Pioneer Award in 2009. He was also one of *OUT Magazine*'s 100 Important Gay People of that year. Picano's most recent work includes *Twelve O'Clock Tales* and *Twentieth Century Unlimited*. *True Stories Too: People and Places From My Past* will be published this year. Picano was openly gay and "out" before the Stonewall Riots and was associated with the early gay political movement (c.f. Jeffrey Schwarz's film: *Vito*). Faced with the threat of what would become the AIDS Epidemic, in 1980, Picano joined eight other men in forming The Gay Men's Health Crisis, the premier organization to combat the disease. Those experiences led him to co-author *The New Joy of Gay Sex* (1992) and *The Joy of Gay Sex*, 3rd Edition (2003), with Dr. Charles Silverstein, addressing men's health issues. The latter title is in its 17th edition and now translated into sixteen languages including Slovenian and Taiwanese. Picano is an adjunct professor of literature at Antioch University, Los Angeles, and he blogs at HuffingtonPost.com. Recent stories, essays, and reviews are free to be read at his website: www.felicepicano.net.

VISITING MY PAPERS AT YALE

Several summers ago I was in New England again, attending a literary conference at The University of Rhode Island, and then doing readings up and down the East Coast for my newest book. Since my rented car would take me right past New Haven, I decided to stop into the Beinecke Rare Book and Manuscript Library at Yale University to look at my papers.

At my age, one begins thinking about collecting what one has carelessly left lying around for decades: at summer cottages, in notebooks, presented to old boyfriends, in hard drives all over the world. I know there are stories, reviews, essays, and poems out there somewhere. I thought maybe someday someone would say, Hey Felice, what about a Collected Poetry? I'd only published two books of poems, *The Deformity Lover* and *Window Elegies*, a chapbook. Another hundred had appeared in print since, the last official one being "His Diagnosis" about my friend, Robert Ferro. After that, poetry seemed no longer possible for me—not for a long time. But there were many earlier poems, poems I'd learned to become a poet writing: learning to become a writer by poetizing. Many I'd left unfinished, hanging, missing a word, a thought not fulfilled. They were inside spiral metal notebooks with chartreuse covers, and those notebooks were at Yale.

Just to clarify, *I* didn't go to Yale; my *papers* went there. I was barely sixteen when I graduated high school. I'd gotten past the rigorous requirements and into Queens College, a free school; I'd even gotten a small scholarship. So that's where I went. I moved to Alphabet City among immigrants and cockroaches, junkies and thieves, and I went to college taking two trains and a bus each way.

However, thanks to scholars George Stambolian, Jonathan Katz and John Boswell, The Beinecke Rare Book and Manuscript Library, which collects American writing groups like the Transcendentalists and Gertrude Stein's Paris circle, collected the works of the Violet Quill Club. So that's where the first half of my papers ended up. I've still got the second half—1988 and after—if anyone's interested.

Before I showed up at Yale, I e-mailed and phoned, warning them I was coming. It was June, with temperatures in the mid-90's Fahrenheit, so I arrived wearing the usual summer gear: shorts, running shoes, and a T-shirt. I was checked in for metal, electronics, cameras, and spyware. My possessions were stowed in a locker. I thought: these people are serious!

I dropped into a large sunlight-filled reading room. At the desk, a woman my age made me fill in a call slip and then told me I had to do it again. "I need two names," she said, sniffily.

"There *are* two names. *Felice* and *Picano*."

"I need a name for the author and your name," she said.

"There they are: Felice Picano and Felice Picano."

I could see her internal computer whirring as she looked at me and she looked at the call slip and then at me again. Her internal computer slowly came to a dead halt. She mumbled: "I'm certain there are no papers here by that person."

"You mean you've lost the eleven cardboard boxes of stuff you guys picked up at my house five years ago?" I asked.

But by then her internal computer was totally kaput: she simply walked away.

People began lining up behind me asking what was the hold-up?

"They've lost all my papers," I said, not believing it possible.

A younger woman eventually showed up pushing an official looking cart and asked what name I was looking for.

"I saw them a few days ago," she said. "What do you need?"

Big sigh of relief.

They weren't yet alphabetized, she said, but they were more or less chronologically sorted, so I asked for the earliest box and one from a middle year. They arrived at length, and I took the boxes to a desk.

Scholars sat all around me literally wearing tweed jackets with leather patches. And those were the women! No wonder the call desk lady had gone AWOL rather than deal with me. As a collected author at the Beinecke, I should have looked like them. Better yet, I should have been dead—for a while.

I found the poems. I very much wanted to but I couldn't correct them because they would only allow me some stubby, tiny soft-lead pencil. So I had the nice young lady photocopy and send them to me at home in L.A. As I'd thought, about a dozen poems looked salvageable with a word or half line changed here or there. Decades later, I could easily see how to fix poems I'd written a dozen times and then simply abandoned in my earlier days.

As I sat there recalling how and when I'd written those poems I looked around and thought: that woman scholar is probably thinking about "the dialectic reification of the masculine principle." While that fellow there is probably contemplating "the hermeneutics of the hetero non-normative."

Could any of them, *any of them*, think what it was like in 1965, as I looked out the grimy backyard window of my $103.00 a month, under-heated, West Village flat and wrote this poem? Could any of them ever imagine what it was like in 1983, when I'd stumbled home from yet another funeral for a dead friend, watched a heedless robin go mad with birdsong, and then penned this other poem? Could anyone in that room comprehend what it was like to have written a totally unexpected, a totally *unprecedented* short story in 1963, to my utter satisfaction? Even knowing that no one would publish it, even knowing that most likely no one would even *read* it because of its gay subject matter? Could anyone there guess what it was like finishing another gay story in 1978 and polishing it to perfection so I could present it, nervously expectant: my first prose reading ever to my peers, to Edmund White and Chris Cox sitting together on the love seat, with Robert Ferro and Michael Grumley stretched on that sofa there, Andrew Holleran on the floor all but hidden, and George Whitmore closest to me, waiting, all of them waiting to be amused, moved, and who knew what else. Shocked? Outraged? Pleased?

I doubt that any of those scholars could or would grasp all that.

Possibly neither can anyone else, except maybe Edmund White and Andrew Holleran . . . if they can remember that fondly, that far.

What follows are eight of the poems I rescued from Yale obscurity. They were written between 1968 and 1972. None were ever published. They are juvenilia, certainly, and my influences are clear: 60's rock music, Elizabethan sonnets, Asian poetry, and art.

COUNTRY-POP SONNET

Some folks say rainbows have an end
Where treasure waits for those who dare.
While others say that life's to share
With a fated love, or one true friend.
But I've seen men who waste their lives
Chasing ideals, that I'd call lies.
And I've know men who'll always try
To turn encounters into wives.
. . . Now, I don't want that abstract gold
Somewhere just around the bend.
And I don't want that dream affair
'Cause dreams will pass, and we'll get old.
I'd just like two clear minds to blend
And when I turn, to see you there.

AFTER A PAINTING BY MU CH'I

Six persimmons
are
soon to be
eternally
dewsweetjuice
fleshcoolfruit
ripe
to eat.

SONG FOR SUSAN

Call up Susan!
She's back from California
Wearing ribbons of despair
In her hair.
She's the Grand Canal of sorrows.
She's forgotten how to care.
She's alone now.

Go see Susan!
How she's changed!
How the 'Frisco mist
And a man she can't name
Have drained out all her light.
She's so tight
Just sitting there,
Wrapping her cares all around her!

Talk to Susan!
Try to tell her
How it's happened once or twice
To everyone half-nice,
Even you,
And her West Coast love affair
Was an adolescent passion—
She won't listen.

Susan! Susan!
She's gotten herself in a love-trap.
All she can see is a road map
Felt tip green lines
Leading eastward,
Leading nowhere.
And she's spent so long in leaving,
She can't believe she's made it

Back to here!
Oh, Susan!

And some months later
You're certain to hear
From several strangers and several near
How Susan's going back.
She's already packed.
To try it just once more
No! Susan!

ADMIRATION

You're so clear
Even the mist knows it.
Look at it hover
And descend all around us:
Weeping eternal slow wetness
Into everything real
That it touches.
What a clammy lover,
What a devourer of color!
Even the crystal is
Damp food for its hunger.
It defends itself
Only from you.
Lifting aloof, it spirals
In angry blue drops—
Nothing like dew—
On the tips of your hair.
What a halo it makes
Under streetlights!

WAITING ROOM

From the moment I bought it
I thought it was a church pew—
All long and dark wood spare:
I saw it distinctly Lutheran—
Until the day I lay down upon it,
Smoking the butt end of a cigarette
And you said I was the picture
Of a small-town traveling hobo
Passing the night asleep on the bench
Of a local railroad station.

Then I knew the idea of a pew
Had brought on great delusions:
For here, clearly, in my living room
To one side of the fireplace,
Opposite the gate-leg table,
Half-reflected in the looking glass—
The bench sits, squat and strong,
Transforming it all
From a home to a true waiting room.

And here I will wait. Isn't that
Why I'm redecorating?
Procrastinating? Despite all my plans
For Big Sur and the Deep South
Of France? Yes. Here I will wait
Until unsated ambitions are filled.
Won't you come and have some tea?
And wait with me?
Wait till your lover has come.
Wait till desires are gone.
Wait until Pluto hits Mars.
Wait, just to wait, in my waiting room?

IS THIS IT, MR. POE?

Man in a crowd
Surrounded by no one
Gets his personal yes
From the overflowing.

Man all alone
Watching the motion
Can't know in advance
Where the tide is going.

So he follows, always follows.
And the sidewalks are
Cardboard stairways to a palace
Always crumbling just
As he gets there. Nothing's
Happening there. Does it
Matter? In your mind's eye,
Isn't life just clatter, just splatter?
Do you follow? Always follow?

Man all alone
You're not eating too well.
You've been missing your sleep
And it's showing.

Man in a crowd
Get away from that glass.
It's *my* reflection there
That you're throwing!

HILLYARD'S COMPLAYNT TO HIS MODEL: A SONNET

Today these hawthorn buds so fill my sight
That surely they had warning you'd desire
To walk with me within this greenwood briar
And, sensing that I perceive but by your light,
To show themselves indifferently white:
Their color I'd compare, and find yours higher.
I think that Nature's folk do all conspire
To blind me quite, that you may beam more bright.
For when I frame you in this garden bower
And picture your curled youth like one rich flower,
Shadows do invade, remind that petals fade,
That vines do wither, this sunlight die in shade.
So more must I labor—to stay this mortal hour
Through all my tinting craft, and passions' power.

MINIATURES

1.
Cats watching shadows
And jumping plaster walls
To scratch at them—
That's what I like about life:
We're not alone
In the greatest delusions.

2.
This world of mine—
How can I best describe it?
A final thrust of dreaming flesh,
A burst of dew,
Then wetness.
After all those complications!

3.
Recognizing infinity
In a swirling moat of coffee
I sat back
And let it take me through. . . .
These instants add up
. . . Eventually.

Q: What are you currently reading?

I'm reading a lot of gay biographies and memoirs. The latter range from the very strong and recommendable —i.e. Glenway Wescott's A Heaven of Words— *to the questionable and even occasional title like that of inaugural poet Richard Blanco. So many gay people want to tell their stories. Whether they are disease and accident survivors, newly or no longer religious, or perhaps just a musician or advertising executive. And I believe that's a good thing, even if the quality is variable. Another trend I'm seeing is the usually but not always academic studies of gay authors and artists of our pre-Stonewall past. This past year saw a batch of heralded books:* Dreadful, *about John Horne Burns,* Farther and Wilder, *about Charles Jackson,* In Bed with Gore Vidal, *and* American Hipster, *about Beat writer/hanger-on Herbert Huncke. These are all long, detailed, books filled with information, really quite solid, and often from mainstream houses. Usually the authors are passionate supporters of their dead subjects. This seems to be an outgrowth of the still bizarre Queer Theory movement which seems to believe that any queer, no matter how minor, is more interesting than anyone leading an out gay and proud life. And so they read as weirdly disjunctive, and sometimes they seem to exist to show merely how duplicitous gay lives were. More interesting by far to me are books like* Fire Island Modernist *about architect Horace Gifford,* Throwaway Boy *about "outsider artist" Henry Darger, and Alysia Abbott's memoir* Fairyland *about growing up with a gay single parent, poet Steve Abbott. In each of these three cases, gay men were doing all they could and at times fighting amazingly difficult odds to be themselves, to lead openly gay lives, and to become artists. Surely these men are the heroes we need. And thanks to these books, heroes that we can now possess in some measure of knowledge and pride.*

JAMES
MITCHELL

ITHURIEL'S SPEAR

JAMES MITCHELL is a San Francisco resident, translator, and writer. He started writing verse in the service of the gay liberation movement in the late 1960's, and he's been at it ever since. James has operated two small presses in San Francisco dedicated to the literary arts. Presently he is the publisher of Ithuriel's Spear, which has plopped forth 24 titles since 2004. In 1969 he started the first gay poetry magazine in San Francisco, and in 1973 he set up Small Press Traffic in the backroom of a bookstore on Castro Street. Remarkably, he made a living for awhile as a musician in the action-packed 1970's, when he was also a founding director of the San Francisco Early Music Society and a music broadcaster on KPFA. He is presently a graduate student in medieval history at San Francisco State, has been a practicing Soto Zen Buddhist since 1971, and, overcoming a passion for fast motorcycles, has now decided upon his eventual reincarnation as a 1957 Oldsmobile convertible (two-tone, white and red, with sidewalls). He has decided to pass the time until then playing old-timey music on his excellent Martin D-28 guitar. Visit his website at plainfeather.blogspot.com.

Q: What poem should we read aloud right now?

"Wales Visitation" by Allen Ginsberg.

JAMES MITCHELL

ON PAUL MARIAH

If medals are ever awarded to small press publishers, a big fat one should go to Paul Mariah, co-publisher of ManRoot Press with Rich Tagett. Paul came to San Francisco after finishing a prison sentence in Illinois for—oh the horror of it—gay sex crimes, and of course he promptly set up a small press upon release in keeping with the revolutionary atmosphere of the times.

I met Paul soon after my own arrival here in 1967, and he was of instrumental value in introducing me to several local poets and artists whom I subsequently published, including Hunce Voelcker, Bill Barber, and also Rich Tagett.

For a couple years, his press and my own impoverished Hoddypoll Press—I thought later that it would have been much better named: Poverty Press—were I think the only ones in town (i.e., within the city limits of San Francisco), and we were certainly the only literary magazines publishing gay poetry, somewhat contemporaneously with Gay Sunshine in Berkeley. Paul wrote poems and slaved constantly over *ManRoot* magazine, and our queer hearts burned with gay revolutionary ardor.

Small press publishing was a terrific hassle in those days. The next step up from mimeographing your stuff was to spend a hundred bucks on a photo offset job, which involved printing off a metal matrix onto sheets of 8.5x11 typewriting paper, then stapling everything together between sheets of cover stock—which you did at home on the living room carpet to save costs. Typesetting was completely unaffordable, so the remaining possibility was an IBM Selectric typewriter, which had these little type-balls facilitating the use of a couple different, but unkerned fonts.

Mistakes were frequent and took forever to remedy, effected through the use of Tipp-ex or the white erasing ribbon installed on the Selectric which never worked properly. It was often infuriating, and it required hours or even days to perform editing tasks that can now be done in a matter of minutes on a computer. The whole enterprise was generally speaking a huge mess—a true Mongolian clusterfuck if there ever was one—but expectations of an approaching gay revolution and our own self-image as underground heroes drove us onward.

Paul lived and worked in his corner apartment at Duboce and Walter, overlooking Duboce Park, whose grassy meadows were still full of dog shit until Harvey Milk famously put an end to it. Paul never ceased toiling behind his IBM Selectric, pausing only when visitors stopped by, and I remember the air in his living room filling blue with cigarette smoke. Out of collegial empathy I wrote the following poem for him, I guess it must be about 40 years ago now.

THE SMALL PRESS LIFE
for Paul Mariah

It was to have been
different.

There were to have been
beautiful editions,
a photograph of the author
on the inside cover,
elegant printing
on cream-colored paper,

and copies to sign
and give away
at crowded readings;

I thought I would
be always on tour,
stopping occasionally
in New York
to consult with
my publishers;

I'd spend a year
in the Caucasus
on some strange fellowship,
and when the Guggenheim
finally arrived, I'd be

at the mouth of the Amazon,
discovering new
botanical specimens,

or in the Himalayas,
exploring
ascetic alternatives,

or I'd be busy
defining novel patterns
of human sexuality

while screwing sheep
on a windy cliff
in Ethiopia.

At a noisy literary party
on Long Island
I'd gain notoriety
by dumping
Norman Mailer
on his ass.

Then I'd marry
my 22-year-old
secretary, gaining
further notoriety
by speaking to no one
for seventeen years.

In extreme old age
I would read
projective verse
at a Presidential inauguration.

And at my death
the I.R.S., Random House,
and Harvard Library

would pick
my white bones clean.

But no.
Instead my life
stutters along
a crazy assembly line

of shamelessly
incomprehensible manuscripts
which generate

drunken typesetting,
messy artwork,
capricious binding,
ephemeral distribution,
and negligible sales.

Correction fluids
of obscure manufacture
have yielded
ineradicable stains
on my pants.

Each time I edit proofs
it occurs to me
that my eyesight
is finally deteriorating.

I am victimized
by the continuing fear
that the postal rates
will increase next month.

Gary Snyder says
of professions, "there
is no other life,"
which I think is correct.

On the other hand,
if alternate proposals
are solicited,
you can bet
I shall not be found
speechless.

On a starry night
I stare upwards
in mute amazement
and wonder where
the big rubber band
which holds
all this together is?

But when the fog
comes in, I am a
champion race-car
driver, assigned
to remain forever
a passenger on an
electric overhead Muni bus.

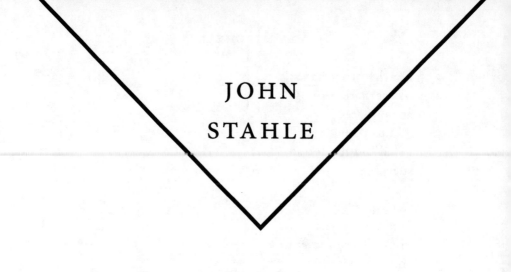

JOHN STAHLE

GANYMEDE

JOHN STAHLE was a freelance graphic designer in New York. He was also a writer and photographer. He published, edited, and designed seven issues of the gay men's literary journal, *Ganymede*. In late 2009, John successfully convinced Bryan Borland to hire him to design and publish *My Life as Adam*, Bryan's first book of poetry. John also talked Bryan into publishing the book under the illusion of an imprint, which would give the book a more professional feel even if the imprint never put out another title. That imprint, under John's guidance, was named Sibling Rivalry Press. John died in 2010, but his influence lives on in the success of *Ganymede*'s heir, *Assaracus*, and in poets such as Matthew Hittinger and Ocean Vuong, who John encouraged and advised. This piece originally appeared in the first issue of *Ganymede*.

NEW YORK IN 1968

In 1968, New York was suspended between two worlds. The old world of Noel Coward and Judy Garland had burnt itself out. But the next world was still forming, the yuppie world of health clubs, Starbucks, e-mail, and million-dollar catboxes. Until that new world gelled, New York slumped in an exhausted, fecund squalor of nearly twenty years while its population contracted. One population never contracted, however: gay men. We believed in New York and kept believing until, once again, it believed in itself. The freedom gay men now enjoy everywhere once existed only in a few cities, and New York offered us the best deal of all.

I first arrived in New York, one fresh homo trainee, on Labor Day weekend in 1968, at the freshman dorm of Fordham University in the Bronx. I dumped my stuff, jumped on the subway, went directly to the Village, walked around, then had my first meal. It was at a diner called Village Den, 12th Street at Greenwich. It's still there, but with a different décor: on that day, I entered a Fifties fantasyland of pink and turquoise vinyl and formica. After my cheeseburger deluxe, I asked directions to the nearby New School, where I felt *sure* Susan Sontag was in the lobby waiting to talk with me.

It was not my first visit. In 1963, we passed through New York on our way to live in Madrid, Spain. As I sat in the backseat on the New Jersey Turnpike, one road sign after another announced bundles of unremembered towns, but then I bolted up in wonder when I finally saw a sign announcing precisely one place: NEW YORK.

Minutes later, the skyline spread out before me like a teasing vision before we dived into the tunnel under the Hudson. Later that visit, I walked through Penn Station three years before its demise, a vast essay in Roman splendor now left to dust and dim lighting. And in our Times Square hotel room, I watched two prime-time game shows, *What's my Line?* and *Masquerade Party,* peopled with glamorous New York celebrities who were paid to go to parties and opening nights. Some I had already met listening to local radio in our car on the way; my father seemed to know these chatty figures and told me all about them.

The next five years were spent as a young nun preparing to take the veil. Sitting in Madrid, I read the *New Yorker* every week and in its pages finally found my role model: staff writer, critic, and profiler Brendan Gill. Gill arrived at the magazine in 1936 directly from Yale and never left. "With the *New Yorker* serving as [his] passport and letter of credit," he went everywhere, met everyone, and wrote it all up in a witty, crystalline style that for me served as the ultimate in *urbanity.* Gill was not just the *New Yorker,* he was *New York.*

I still wanted to meet Susan Sontag, and three months after that first diner meal, I did, because her only contribution was herself, relentlessly promoted like a new brand of toothpaste, not the wildly

unreliable blather she published. But I was never curious to meet
Gill, though I saw him often enough on television. To me, Gill *was*
his writing; his person just did the typing and the traveling and the
talking.

In 1968, there were precisely four gay neighborhoods. Most self-
identified homos lived in the West Village because that's where the
best cruising was—the same reasoning that prompted observant Jews
to live within walking distance of a synagogue. Chelsea did not exist
yet, although West Village rents, commercial and residential, would
soon send pioneers there. The East Village, except for a couple of
blocks around St. Marks and one very unkempt W.H. Auden, had
been annexed by Puerto Rico and the drug trade. That left a bunch of
opera queens in the west 70s and snooty wallets in the east 70's. Plus
one tribe who for some reason insisted on living in Jackson Heights,
Queens. Total: four gay ghettos. The lesbians were busy saving Park
Slope for white people. Other fine spots, like Brooklyn Heights and
Astoria, simply slept. And *nobody* heard of Williamsburg.

In 1968, a culturally aware homo still perceived in the city the
long shadow of the Twenties, when modernism was launched: neon
lights, radio, magazines, advertising, vast subway systems, movies. In
that decade, half the city went up and complex mass media rose with
it, each promoting the romance and glamour of the other.

Before 1968, being gay meant going to live theater, which often
cost no more than movies, and whose creative center, from Tennessee
Williams to Rodgers and Hammerstein, was still Broadway. By
1968, it was all over except the exceptions. Instead of Mary Martin
and Ethel Merman, we got *Hair,* then *Chorus Line.* Interest shifted to
off-Broadway, but pickings were thin there too, except for the new
theater devoted to Shakespeare in Central Park. And yet, amateur
theater was in great shape: aspiring actors who never went to drama
school could actually perform Chekhov or Molière in little church
groups with useful results. All gone now.

Dance fared better. Balanchine moved to Lincoln Center and
filled a new, bigger stage with the gems of a very busy maturity, and
Jerome Robbins left Broadway to work with him there. The British
Royal Ballet visited every spring, with a legendary lineup, directed
by Frederick Ashton himself. American Ballet Theatre had staged the
first American *Swan Lake* successfully and would soon hire two great

Russian defectors of lasting influence.

Opera fared even better. Two years into its new house at Lincoln Center, the Met was simply chockablock with divinities—nearly every great star then singing, with conductors to match—while its scrappy cousin, New York City Opera, offered Beverly Sills and Plácido Domingo. Across the plaza at the Philharmonic, Leonard Bernstein's tenure was nearly over, and all buzz focused on the audacious programming of his replacement, Pierre Boulez.

In 1968, Judy Garland, our finest link with that old world, had one more year to live; the following summer, her funeral drew tens of thousands of queens uptown to view the casket. After standing in the hot line all afternoon, some returned downtown to their favorite dive, The Stonewall, for a drink and a cry. They were in a *state*. The police chose the wrong night for another of their vicious raids with beatings; this time, the queens fought back and launched gay liberation around the world. Judy's death freed us, and we weren't kidding.

Josephine Baker, another old object of camp affection, performed her last concert in New York a little later, in 1973 at Carnegie Hall. By then the thin high voice from the 1930's recordings had given way to a throaty, slick mezzo, and she dressed like a Las Vegas show girl: very high heels, one-piece bathing suit in spangled silver, big headdress. That's how she dressed when she walked out to the front of the Carnegie stage and looked down. The entire front row, end to end, had been taken by drag queens dressed *exactly* like her at that moment. It took a while for Josephine to recover her composure and this disconcerting gay vision was what she took back to Paris.

Not all the news was good in 1968. Architecture delivered the worst body blow to the city. In the Fifties and Sixties, New York was enslaved by the dark arts of Bauhaus and Le Corbusier, a style of staggering mediocrity and perversion unique in world history. Everything that worked in urban planning since 1850 was now blandly denied by weasels who made their careers contradicting reality. They gained control of this trade by closing their fists around its two testicles, training schools and the critical establishment. They squeezed and to this day are still squeezing. Bolshevism came to architecture (and classical music) just as it came to politics. An early modernist manifesto actually said it: *We know best.* Even today, the architectural critic of the *New York Times,* a young man named Nicolai Ouroussoff, defends modernism with the obtuse fervor of an old Bolshevik. The public had the last laugh in suburbia, where they shat on it, but in New York it was like living in Romania under the Communists. Now, in a bitter irony, young architects think 1960 style is so cool it deserves revival, and one new building after another shows that nobody learned a thing from the cold, bland crap of that period. Post-modernism was laughed out of court by those squeezing the two testicles, but in the few years clients were allowed such choice, architecture in the city miraculously returned to the conversation of the Twenties.

In 1968, every college student read Jane Jacobs' *Life and Death of Great American Cities,* which re-taught truths about urban values modernists had denied. By then, whole acres of varied, dynamic, jumbled, funky, and irreplaceable urban fabric had been destroyed for Corbu's vision of blunt brick towers sitting on bald lawns. A teeming square block would be cleared for one corporate building whose owners refused to rent their ground floor to shops the public actually used, leaving us to walk along dead sidewalks with pristine bank branches and 60-foot loading docks instead. Jacobs' points are now so accepted, so well re-learned, that there is no point in reading her anymore—except for those obtuse young architects who should be forced to.

But architecture was not the only modernism being renounced. After a brief hegemony by Americans like Hemingway, readers in 1968 had turned to European voices of deeper, more resonant culture: Jorge Luis Borges, who offered a rich mélange of old-world fantasy with walk-ons by gauchos and tango dancers; Vladimir Nabokov, who carried his White Russia with him as he spent summers sampling American motels armed with a butterfly net; or the strange fashion for Hermann Hesse's dank pre-war German symbolism. Readers swarmed over comparative religion and mythology: Mircea Eliade, Alan Watts, Joseph Campbell. In the Sixties, the reading tastes of urban literates opened like a glorious young flower, establishing new trends still being mined intensively today.

The Sixties were also paperback heaven: hardly anything cost more than $2.50. Key lit player: New Directions, who introduced Borges in 1964 with the compilation *Labyrinths,* plus so many others, from

Djuna Barnes to Dylan Thomas, a backlist that is still indispensable. Signet, Penguin Classics (whose paper turned brown after only a year), and Dover Books were also ubiquitous. Top scholarly studies were issued by the paperback houses Mentor and Harper Torchbooks and sold for less than two dollars. Now, university presses issue their own paperbacks at obscene prices few students can readily afford.

Movies underwent the sharpest change between New York's old and new worlds. Before television, most movies played one week in big downtown palaces and one week in neighborhood theaters. Then they vanished. Yes, you could rent a 16mm print to show in a church basement, but how many people did that? Back then, movies were as ephemeral as live theater, and stars had to keep pumping out new product to avoid oblivion.

But by 1968, Manhattan was dotted with busy, sophisticated revival houses staffed by real cineastes: Thalia, Elgin, Theatre 80 St. Marks, Regency, New Yorker, Gramercy, Carnegie Hall Cinema, and most prestigious of all, the basement theater of the Museum of Modern Art. Every New Yorker from that period counts nights spent in these magic caves as precious to their cultural and social lives; Woody Allen and other filmmakers worked the experience into their films. Revival houses started here around 1945; their promotion of old and foreign films, followed by television and then video rentals, transformed a narrowly national, ephemeral medium into an international archival medium. Any aspiring filmmaker could now learn the entire history of cinema from home, lounging in his underwear. In 1941, *Citizen Kane* played three weeks in three theaters in three cities, then vanished—a total flop—until in the mid-Fifties revival houses and television made it the great classic it is today, the classic of a medium that now forgets no film.

A day in the life of a homo, circa 1968? Depended on your tastes. For the sex compulsive who moved to the Village for cruising, most nights were spent walking the streets with the fervor of sailors haunting the docks in Genet's *Querelle*. The sex pig would take his trick home around the corner, have fun until dawn, nap briefly after tossing him out, then go to work from nine to five, finally crashing on the weekend, helped when needed by caffeine or something stronger. The more moderate homo would save his outreach for the weekend; each of our four neighborhoods had a selection of gay bars. Shop, screw, sleep late, then test your trick's gentility and conversation over a 2 PM brunch—a fashion we created. (When people ask me what separates gays from straights physically, I explain that we have a second stomach just for brunch.)

In the old New York world, gay bars were breeding grounds for blackmail, and careful homos relied instead on a network of private parties and introductions. That network still worked for us in 1968, but many gay boys still preferred to sample fresh meat in the squalor of dive bars. For the gay world, before and since, has always been democratic: no one cares about your class or place of origin. To succeed in gay life, you need only maintain a flat stomach and be brunchable. Trim and genteel; every other trait, even hair on the back, has a niche market.

Back then we were very direct in wanting action, right now and without fuss, and for our chosen targets we required only a hole and a smile. Today, we edge closer and closer to women: we want sex from inside a relationship, we are picky, and in our dating we make 'em wait. Gay men do not pay for their dates, so right off we are free of the principle source of rage among hetero men who spend their lives paying, even when she makes more, and still get cold-shouldered.

Gay life seldom gets credit for its efficient social mobility: a boy who grew up poor, rough, but attractive needed only to meet a white homo lover and be transformed thereby, ready to spend and consume in the tasteful cocoon of the urban gay middle class. In 1968, so many black men hitched their wagons to better-paid white men for that purpose; nowadays, they tend to stay with their own, and their places are taken by Hispanic immigrants. You rarely saw a blond take another blond as a lover; he always favored an opposite; we called that *salt and pepper*. In 1968, the salt was still WASP suburban blond, and the pepper was swarthy urban Jewish; soon the pepper would shift to poor Puerto Rican and then to accented South American arrivals. Our social mobility engine is still a big contributor to the city's middle class and all the Pottery Barns it patronizes.

A tectonic change in the gay community was just gathering force in 1968. Homos arrived here unafraid of blackmail and eager to sample all the old outlaw vices—in their own, safer way, without being corrupted and debased by them. One market in particular shifted to accommodate this ambition: gay bathhouses. New, clean, well-run and specifically gay bathhouses opened around then, most notably the Club Baths (now Lucky Cheng's), a chain from Miami. Rooms available for eight hours, health-club standards for showers and hot tubs, shag carpet, smooth piped-in music, two-for-one admissions, and a dark orgy room with plastic-sheeted bunk beds for the cash-challenged . . . suddenly gay suburbanites could enjoy the same steamy pleasures that used to be found only in creepy old Russian or Jewish settings where gay men were only tolerated. At the Club, you were escorted to your room or locker by another gay boy, perhaps one you knew; you relaxed in a TV lounge chatting with homos instead of skulking about. Later, the Club even built a glassed-in winter garden with plastic greenery and recorded bird sounds! And everywhere, showers, bathrooms, clean towels for the asking, and mouthwash to keep your *bouche* fresh and clean. By the Seventies, the gay bathhouse market had divided into three: the clean, safe one at the Club, Man's Country and a couple of others, opened just for nice homos; harder-core spots, like St. Mark's, catering to the sex compulsives (nice boys did poorly there; sex pigs could sniff out moderation and reject it in a blink); and the remnants of straight-run creepy baths, now visited only by pot-bellied poops like Truman Capote who would find themselves shunned with a shudder at the Club. The gay mainstream spent the Seventies trying this fashion. Then, around 1980, we all noticed a sudden drop-off at all the nice baths: one Saturday was half the business, then the next visit half again, until by the onset of AIDS the nice baths were already gone, the victims of a consensus: we tried it; now let the niche market have it again.

I met all my friends at the Club Baths. The reason was simple: no games. Either your target was interested or he was not; you checked all the goods before handling; time was spent making love, not teasing across smoky rooms over liquor. For the more promising, a shower, sauna, or hot tub together, maybe a little TV or a chat on plush sofas. The most promising you brought home and then admired, re-clothed, over brunch the next day. Love, or at least *like,* blossomed efficiently in this setting. I had no tolerance for the ennui of gay bars, and still don't.

On my last day in town for 1968, I packed to take the train home for Christmas break. But first I wanted to fortify myself by visiting my two favorite bookshops. The night before, an enormous snowstorm had covered New York in velveteen white, and now a dreamy quiet reigned everywhere. First I stopped at the Gotham Book Mart, the legendary bookstore in midtown. Gotham opened in 1920, and in its sacred space that decade was still alive. As I clumped in, founder Frances Steloff was having tea in a book-lined alcove with one of her white-haired girlfriends. Upstairs, near the little magazines, a notice announced with great pride that Gotham would soon sell a limited-edition print by Andy Warhol—signed by the artist! Someone sat nearby doing the signing, so I went over. It wasn't Andy Warhol, just a pimply student intern. *Caveat emptor*.

Next stop: the Eighth Street Bookstore. Crunching through the snow of the West Village, I sniffed a different wood fire every few yards, a delicious surprise winter still offers me there every year. In 1968, all the kids wanted to look like Bob Dylan on his record albums, walking down Bleecker Street in a navy pea coat, thick scarf theatrically wound around his neck, and pipe-stem, boot-flare jeans.

I bought enough books to keep New York culture in front of me until I returned. Back at the freshman dorm, everybody was playing the new Beatles' *White Album*. I took my bag and went down to Penn Station. It was not the awesome civic edifice I first tiptoed through in 1963. That was gone, replaced with a bland strip mall stuck underground. "We used to arrive in New York like kings," commented architectural historian Vincent Scully with great bitterness. "Now we scuttle like rats through a hole in the ground." New York in 1968.

LEAVING EARTH

I grind my eyes
to diamonds
breaking quartz and crystal
on wind.
My feet weave among
closely set trees.
I am unlife
for hours and days.

Subject of knives,
your confusion is my history.
There is a hole in the sky
where pain escapes.
Its red eye blinks.
Enter it quickly:
a sliding moon.

My heart is stunned *I am I am I am.*
Like a stillborn child
I have decided not to breathe.

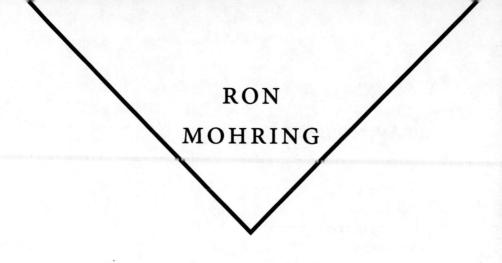

SEVEN KITCHENS PRESS

RON MOHRING founded Seven Kitchens Press in 2007 and had absolutely no idea what he was getting into. Sixty chapbooks later, he's still terribly excited about this project. Six of his poems in this issue are from a chapbook-in-progress, *Catches & Stays*, and originate with lines borrowed from Seven Kitchens authors. His full-length collection, *Survivable World*, won the Washington Prize. He lives in Lewisburg, Pennsylvania.

Q: What responsibility does the poet have to the gay community?

I don't necessarily think of the "gay community" as a measure, but I do feel a strong loyalty to truth-telling and representing my place in a diverse queer tribe. We must tell our own stories.

Q: What makes you proud when you think about Seven Kitchens?

I recently sent an open letter to our authors to update everyone on the state of our budget and production schedule, but also to reaffirm my commitment to the 7KP family. Their overwhelmingly generous response made me realize what a huge accomplishment I've managed in just six years: such a strong and diverse body of work!

ALL AFTERNOON

I hid in the campus library with books I'd pulled
      for their titles
or the lines of a random poem inside, trailing my fingers
      along their spines,
selecting them solemnly, loving their company, how they
      waited to be found.
I had slipped away from work, from home, and where else
      to go but here,
the upper floor, the quiet corner near the abused art books,
      the wide window
facing south toward the river with its one mountain, its gulls
      flashing like windblown
scraps of paper? I read and read, copying lines and sometimes
      whole poems
into my notebook; I could do this all day and not tire of it, though
      I couldn't help
but watch the stealthy men slip up the corridor, pause to drink
      at the fountain
then glance around before entering the men's room. I counted
      the minutes
they waited; I watched them go; I could have been invisible.
      I thought this might
be how the dead must feel: to wait, brimming with longing
      but faceless,
voiceless, the way a book depends on human connection
      to become
complete, a closed circuit. Of all the furtive men that afternoon,
      just one nodded,
and though I nodded back, speechless with hunger, I understood
      I was nothing
but a witness, and the humming lighting seemed
      to seep inside
the desk's sharp edges, which brightened and shook into
      a piercing wind
that filled the room and blew me hollow as a winter reed.

AND GO

Another clunky fiction of seduction, another story
someone can't keep straight. Truth is, doesn't matter
who we say we are. This one calls himself Pete
Stone, probably misses the redundancy. My mind's
not wholly on the task but his hand on my head tells me
I'm doing fine. Motorcycle helmet glinting on the coffee
table, shirt peeled off and flung across the Windsor
chair. Quizzed later on the décor, he'd be sure
to fail: he's totally into the vintage porn flickering
across the room. Which mouth am I? Bent to my eager
labor, I register the long moan signaling the payoff's
near. On this rock I reaffirm my faith in the brotherhood
of moment's notice, anointed by the quick and not-yet-dead.

Italicized passage from Ed Madden,
"For what I assume is membership," *Nest* (2010)

DEAR JOHN,

I'd sooner chew the cords
of small appliances. I'd rather gnaw
my foot off at the ankle, jab a sharp stick
in each eye. Better to yank the car to the shoulder
and shove my tongue up a dead doe's ass
than kiss that mouth of yours. Better to pour
horse piss in my ear than listen to that yammer.
Get me a witness; bring me a funnel. Better,
a funnel cloud. Better to leap into that whirling shredder
than stay one damn more minute here with you.

Italicized passage from Terry Kirts,
"Against Cilantro," *To the Refrigerator Gods* (2010)

FORCING NARCISSUS

You look like a self-portrait but feel like a mirror:
you need us to know
how you are. Resplendent in whatever,
topped off with that faux-
casual do: if we touched your hair would it shatter?
Your fuck-me-or-don't-
I-don't-care slouch, your coyly jaded demeanor?
You can't keep your eyes
from flicking toward each new arrival: potential suitor?
Threat to your domain?
Fresh unsullied tongue to maybe plumb and plunder
your stunning ass? You
never know unless you ask. Honey, please. Come down from your
silly high horse. Life's hard
enough without this inscrutable posing. There, there.

Italicized passage from RJ Gibson,
"With You as Vincent," *Scavenge* (2010)

IT WAS NOTHING

Just tall enough to raise the hammer but never able
to drop it on the gaping heads of whiskered catfish,
those sad comics in their too-tight suits we had
to shuck with pliers, their beady eyes rolling in bewilderment.
Of course it wasn't, of course my neighbor knew better
than to take me fishing though I begged him, of course
the worms writhed in something other than pain,
though it looked like pain, though he said it was nothing
when the cat finned him good and the blood seeped from
his wrist. Blue boat rocking on the pond, sun beating
our backs. Green heron clamped like a bundle of rags
to the half-sunken log, dragonflies lighting on our rods
then flicking off again, the care he took so natural, inevitable,
and hadn't I latched onto him, wasn't this what I wanted without
knowing it? Dazed, acquiescent, carried out of my fevered body
and into the cloaking shade of the dumbstruck trees?

Italicized passage from Boyer Rickel,
["a friend confides she chose the flat"], *reliquary* (2009)

RON MOHRING

SHUTTERS

What shutters the relentless battering begins to warp and give, the way
the floorboards seethed, softening their hold before being taken.
Weeks later, driving through the now-cleared underpass
that had taken a colleague's car—she'd climbed to the roof only
to be attacked by a fizzing mat of floating fire ants—we note
the wrack line of branches and debris, dotted with bright trash.
To return to the scene, to know that one survived while others,

equally randomly, did not: what does this gain? What shutters
the relentless voice insisting we don't deserve this fragile grasp,
this second chance? Green spearing through the mud. We're not
so easily mended. When she saw the water rising, her only
thought was who would find and feed her cats. I ask
gently, keep the story on her, my own shuttering mistaken
for a truer concern. We live. We live in doubt. We drive away.

Italicized passage from Lisa Sewell,
"The Corrections," *Long Corridor* (2009)

WHO CANNOT

He is wasting his time trying to sing. He strips
rose hips, brilliant in November rain. Stuffed
into damp pockets, found shrunken blackened later
so why steal ever—bright bits flaming against winter,
glancing thought that these are good but for what?
Rose fruit. Hips. Ships packed for some tomorrow.
For the birds, what meager meat. A casual thief,
he pockets seeds, bits of bark, cicada husks so bleached
and whisper-thin it's unthinkable they might have ferried
such raucous bodies from the earth. He walks and walks,
feet numb in wet sneakers, white plume of breath escaping,
hovering, nothing but water and air.

Italicized passage from Jeff Oaks,
"Who Cannot Read This," *Shift* (2010)

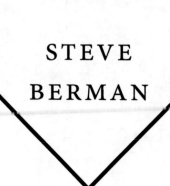

STEVE
BERMAN

LETHE PRESS

STEVE BERMAN sold his first story when he was seventeen. He has continued to write, publish, and edit ever since. He founded Lethe Press in 2001. Lethe specializes in LGBT books of speculative fiction and the strange—literally queer. This story for *Assaracus* is just the latest in a series of fictional, autobiographical, and avuncular vignettes. He resides in southern New Jersey.

Q: Who, writing now, excites you?

I think, in terms of queer stuff, my favorite "new" authors are: Sean Eads (The Survivors) who has also written some amazing short fiction including—my personal favorite—Oscar Wilde fighting off zombies; the Thai author Benjanun Sriduangkaew is terrific; and Sunny Moraine has also told some incredible genderqueer tales.

Q: What is the most rewarding thing about running Lethe?

The opportunity to publish authors who would be overlooked by other small (and large) presses. In 2014 we have O. Henry Award-winner Keith Banner's new collection (hard to believe he isn't being pursued by a larger house, but the material is gay. . . .) and Jeff Mann's sequel to his best-selling Civil War novel. The authors are so gracious. It makes me feel good.

TELLTALE SCENTS

April winds tugged at me and brought the stink of fresh urine and redolent cologne. My eyes teared yet I saw the dirt and shadows of Philadelphia and the dying man on the asphalt. I heard his screams. He lay in a puddle of his own blood that leaked from the hole where his genitals once were. His arms twitched, fingers trembling near the wound, as if he meant to dip his fingertips into the last dribble of the arterial spray. The toes of my shoes already were crimson as I stood over him.

The overpowering stench went past the arm with which I covered my lower face and ignited my memories. Decades back to a summer afternoon on the Chesapeake Bay, aboard a small sailboat with a man I have tried never to think about since then.

Can you Canoe? That had been the advertising slogan.

"Uncle" Artie was not related by blood to my parents. But he was my father's co-worker at the bank, and they both daydreamed of owning a boat of their own. One of them decided that sailing lessons in Annapolis would be a solid step toward their shared goal. At fourteen, I was the only kid available to give a socially acceptable veneer to the project. Artie and his wife Eileen did not have children. They had terriers. My sisters were some combination of grown-up, married, and pregnant.

Uncle Artie got a perm a year before my father did. He wore open-necked shirts. He stank like a bad cookie, a sickly vanilla smell that I soon learned was a cheap cologne called Canoe. I remember Uncle Artie showing me how a man was meant to tip the open bottle of *eau de cologne* onto a fingertip and then brush that finger across the neck. His touch had lingered along my throat and the momentary chill of the cologne's alcohol evaporating was not what made me shudder.

His wife's hair had looser curls than her husband's perm and she reeked of gin and never went out on the water but stayed on shore, drinking martinis at the yacht club bar.

Most of the sailing instructors were local college kids earning money during summertime. My memory renders them as handsome Ken and Barbie dolls wearing polos and shorts and boat shoes without socks—each blond and tan and seamless.

If the instructor was a guy, and my mother wasn't aboard, we were encouraged to piss over the side of the boat. I was the very definition of pee-shy. I cannot recall using a urinal until I went off to college. The thought of catching a glimpse of another man's penis was both thrilling and frightening, like catching a glimpse of a shark's fin breaking the surface of the water. I would have liked to have seen any of the instructors' penises, if only to discover whether they were tan and surrounded by sun-bleached pubes. But the instructors knew to pee at the very prow, where they were unlikely to be ogled, while Uncle Artie went for starboard.

The bone-white stripe of zinc oxide on his thick nose might as well have helped his aim as protected from sunburn. Uncle Artie unzipped his fly and seemed to take an inordinate amount of time pulling his dick out of his shorts. "You gotta make sure you have a firm grip on the weiner. And don't forget the shake. That's the best part," Uncle Artie said.

I had anticipated that one day I would get a phone call from either my mother or my sister telling me that my nephew was dead. A gay kid squatting in one of the worst parts of Philly was one step away from a tragic ten-second report on the nightly news. When the expected call came, though, tragedy had devolved to melodrama: he was alive in the hospital. The mugger had not been sated with an old iPhone, his messenger bag, and a few crumpled bills; he broke my nephew's left eye socket and a few ribs.

Zach had only been conscious long enough to mutter the word "Uncle" to the doctors in the emergency room. I wondered if my sister somehow blamed me because of this.

That summer had been a hot one, the sun glaring down at the water. I did not skimp on drinking from the thermos my mother thrust at me before casting off. But the breeze cooled any sweat and the lemonade went down my throat straight for my bladder, which wanted to burst by the time we had tacked about; sailing seemed nothing more than the slowest way to travel invented. A crew at the dock called to us to help secure the boat by wrapping lines around the cleats and dropping bumpers. Artie told me to help them as he followed the instructor to the club.

And before I could refuse, one of the crew—one more handsome college kid—had handed me the line and was talking knots while I was aware of my full bladder's terrible ache. After the boat was secure, I hobbled to the bathrooms.

Inside, I faced the urinals. I glanced toward the single. The urinals felt too exposed even with the weak overhead fluorescent lighting. Heading for the stall, I heard sounds. In the span between door and concrete floor, I saw the worn rubber soles of deck shoes. Someone kneeling in front of the toilet. Someone seasick. I don't remember touching the stall door. I wouldn't have. Never. And yet it swung inward and I saw the instructor standing astride the toilet and Uncle Artie on his knees, his mouth buried in the instructor's crotch, so deep it was like watching a lamprey feed. Nothing sexual whatsoever despite the look on the instructor's face, which was pained.

A warm stream ran down my leg. My bladder released.

I basically did what you were not supposed to do and jumped into the water by the docks, which was full of barnacles, debris, and crabs. I spit out what foul water reached my mouth. My excuse was clumsiness. My reward was a tetanus shot.

I never told my parents about Uncle Artie. I never needed to, as my father took another job soon after that summer of sailing.

I cannot sleep at nights. I keep hearing thoughts and they won't be silent. Loneliness. Men from the past I wish I had stayed with or that they had offered to stay with me.

My doctor prescribed pills on top of anti-anxiety meds. Little things that should help me fall asleep. Mirtazapine. Only I ended up waking up in the middle of the night with my underwear soaked and the bed wet. I sniffed—it lacked the pungency of urine and at first I thought it was sweat, though that seemed ridiculous. Night after night, and I had to sleep atop thick towels. And one night, as I was easing into sleep—*Can you Canoe?*—I felt the urine dribble out of my penis. Only two percent of folk using Mirtazapine have nighttime incontinence. I was finally one of the elite.

The doctor switched my med to Trazodone, a pill that looks like it was made by a geometry teacher with a love of triangles—I could have one, two, or even all three wedges if I needed it. A side effect is priapism, an erection lasting too long for comfort's sake. But did that happen to me? No.

I wet the bed every night. Or don't sleep. And I have to sleep.

I'll always be lonely. I can never share my bed with anyone.

Without meaning to, I found the guy who beat up my nephew. Actually, I wish I hadn't. He was in the alley a few blocks from the derelict tenement where Zach was squatting. If the breeze hadn't blown the odors my way, if the sun had not been high overhead, I might not have gone down there.

Zach's iPhone, its glass shiny and wet, but not with the mugger's blood. My nose knew the puddle was pure cologne leaking from a broken bottle in the stolen messenger bag. I stepped closer to the dying mugger. I hawked what phlegm I could muster and let it drip, so slow, so slow, from my open mouth onto his eyes, which were beginning to glaze.

The phone rang. I didn't touch it, but the speaker came on. *Hey, kiddo, can you Canoe? Did you remember to shake? That's the best part.*

I shuddered. I ran.

Uncle Artie gave my father a bottle of Canoe for Hanukkah. But my father never wore cologne—he preferred expensive watches and shoes—so the bottle sat atop his dresser alongside the leather box filled with old coins, cufflinks, and the mysterious white plastic tabs somebody—my dad?—eventually explained were collar stays. I waited until it had a fine coating of dust before pouring the entire bottle down the sink. I was seventeen and the bathroom reeked as though a barbershop had collapsed down the drain. I kept the hot water tap on, tried adding rubbing alcohol until the smell had evaporated.

It took almost two weeks before my father noticed the missing bottle.

How did Zachary get his hands on Canoe? But then I remember my mother saying that, in the days following my father's death, my sister and nephew went through Dad's dresser drawers—my sister was

ASSARACUS

looking for one of the gold watches (long since sold) and my nephew supposedly wanted a memento. Could my father have bought another bottle? Had my mother replaced the lost Canoe?

In the hospital, bandages covered half of Zachary's face. I told my sister and mother to go eat something and I sat down to watch over Zach.

The room's landline phone rang.

Have you finally learned how to aim, kiddo? The voice of a dead man. Without a trace of static, as if 4G signals could cross the border between sanity and craziness. *Remember the shake. Zachary loves to Canoe.*

You're dead.

Hey, I missed you. But your nephew loves the attention. Like the instructor. You saw how I gobbled him down. Or the schwartza that hit my boy.

He's not yours.

He loves it when I make him shake, kiddo. Don't fool yourself.

The phone's dial tone returned. Had I imagined the call?

The ring of the phone had happened though, because it woke Zach.

"Hey, Zee. How are you feeling?"

"Uncle Steve . . . was that him?" His words spoken with swollen lips and a dry tongue came out as a rasp, but each might as well have been shouted.

My legs felt unsteady, so I sat down in the chair beside the bed.

"Tell me. Tell me what happened."

He started crying, tears flowing from his visible eye, perhaps soaking the gauze on the other—do tears still happen if your eye socket is broken? Or would that eye always be dry, I had to wonder, and the thought made him seem all the more tragic.

"He visits me. A few weeks ago I just was crushed. I mean, the entire building, I get food for everyone. But there's never enough in the dumpsters and I have to keep looking and looking and I'm so tired. And even if you find food for them, you have to listen to them and their lives are so bad and I just wanted a few minutes to forget. To remember when life was easier.

"And I remembered Pop-Pop's cologne. And so I sat in the corner and undid the top and sniffed. Wasn't like huffing. I never even remember him wearing it—"

"—He didn't. Thank God."

"And that's when I first heard him."

"Uncle Artie."

"And he said such sweet things to me. But when the cologne was gone, so was the voice. So I had to get more. It's so cheap. You can buy it under five dollars on Amazon. And I OD'd on his attention. I had enough where I could feel him. Him feeling me.

"And I started to forget to get the food, and the neighbors pounded on my door and so I rushed out, but it was late. And this guy jumped me. Beat me up. Took my phone."

I decided to risk going to my nephew's apartment in the badlands of the city.

How could my nephew live in such squalor? What had driven him from suburbia? I felt that I no longer had any grasp on the man he had become and I was intruding on a stranger's territory.

The apartment was a studio. Not a single wall lacked a crack, holes, or filthy streaks of what I suspected might be mold. The carpet looked so dingy I wasn't sure what the original color must have been. The one closet door hung askew on one hinge.

On a nightstand beside a crumpled mattress on the floor, a traditional goldfish bowl filled with water rested atop a paperback of Chomsky's *Selected Readings*. Inside a black fish swam in circles over a bed of colorful tiny rocks. Round-bellied, the fish had bulbous eyes, a breed I remember being fascinated by as a child but could no longer remember what they were called. A strip of masking tape on the glass bore the fish's name: *Othello*. I opened the tiny container of food beside the bowl and dropped a pinch of flakes onto the water's surface. Othello, a gourmand, gobbled each before it could drift down to the bottom.

The familiar smell grew stronger as I approached the bathroom. *Can you Canoe?*

The art-deco cologne bottles cluttered the top of the toilet tank, the little flat spots on the chipped porcelain sink meant for soap, piled on the grimy floor tiles. If not a bottle, then a recycled plastic spritzer bottle with the label of whatever cleaning solution peeled away.

I began pouring them out. Seventeen again. But the smell was too much, too many bottles. The bathroom mirror fogged as I turned on the hot water tap; the cold would not turn. I was scared that letters would form on the mirror. *Can you Canoe?*

I asked my mother about what happened with Uncle Artie and Aunt Eileen. I assumed both were dead like most of my parents' peers. She knew where Eileen was buried—they had gone to her funeral at Haym Salomon cemetery. We all owned plots there, though my father was cremated and his wooden box rests in honor atop a bureau.

On the hour drive to the cemetery the Beach Boys came on the radio. I thought of sailing, and stabbed the button to change stations to NPR.

I told the manager of Haym Salomon that I was a friend of Uncle Artie—saying the words made bile rise in my throat—and wanted to pay my respects. Jews don't bring flowers, we place rocks on the bronze markers. The manager found in his ledger Eileen's plot but there was no grave for Artie. I asked if Artie was still alive. He was kind enough to share with me the man's last known address, a nursing home in Levittown.

Trazodone and Mirtazapine are not very toxic, according to the Internet. There's no way I can guess the right dosage to kill a man. I grind up all the pills I have and dump the powder into one of the orange plastic prescription containers.

Nursing homes may claim to be cognizant of security but, really, they're not. Much like the independent-living community my mother lives in, you cannot just walk into the building but have to be buzzed in—but since none of the occupants in this building are competent, the office needs to let you inside. You speak at the window.

The workers at nursing homes are tired and worn down by the demands of their charges. Much like Zachary. And so a smile and patience and kind words are a panacea to their frayed nerves. I did not even need to show identification to be allowed inside to visit Uncle Artie.

The hallways are painted a faded yellow. Scratched wooden rails for the residents to hold on to are everywhere.

The nurse who leads me to his room tells me he suffered a series of strokes before and during his stay. He sits in a wheelchair near the window. He's slumped to one side and the soft blanket that covers much of him looks like it was meant for an infant's crib, not an old man. I can see the bottom of a plastic bag by the chair's side. It is filled with urine. He has a catheter.

His eyes look at me though his face cannot move and there's a bit of frothy saliva at the corner of his mouth. He lacks the smell of cheap vanilla. No cologne. Just the scent of evacuated bowels.

My phone rings. I ignore it.

I close the door. I expect to get caught, of course. They've made my work easy by leaving a lunch tray with a container of apple sauce. I dump the powder onto the pureed fruit and stir it in with a plastic spoon. I do all this in front of him, so he can see and know.

Of course, old men do die every day. And Jews don't always bother with autopsies. I have to shove the spoon into his mouth. He cannot resist the urge to swallow. I try not to think what he has swallowed in the past . . . the instructor, from Zachary, what he did to the mugger.

And his eyes close just as I see the blanket tenting at his crotch. Trazodone, you fickle bastard, why him and not me? That stubby dick is like a middle finger lifted at me in derision. But then, with the catheter in him, perhaps that erection isn't so pleasing. An ounce of constant pain before he falls asleep forever would be fitting.

When I'm finished, I slip the spoon in my pocket, wipe the door handle with one of the paper napkins from the lunch tray, and leave the nursing home with my head down.

It's raining and by the time I reach my car I'm soaked.

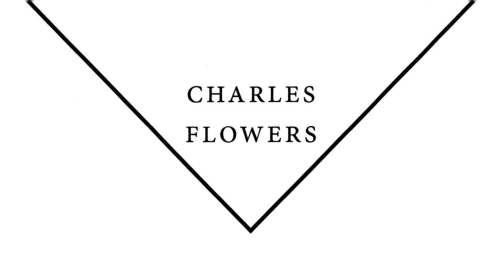

CHARLES FLOWERS

BLOOM

CHARLES FLOWERS graduated Phi Beta Kappa from Vanderbilt University and received his MFA in Poetry from the University of Oregon. His poems have appeared in *Gulf Coast*, *Barrow Street*, *Indiana Review*, and *Puerto del Sol*. Flowers is the founding editor of *BLOOM*, a journal for lesbian and gay writing, which celebrates its tenth year in 2014 (www.bloomliteraryjournal.org). After twenty years in Tennessee and twenty years in New York, Charles now calls Los Angeles home, with his husband and two dogs.

Q: What have you learned from publishing *BLOOM*?

I've learned so much, but the key lesson is that there continues to be a role for publications like BLOOM—to bring new work by queer writers into the hands of readers, literally as a print publication. It brings me joy to do this, and to join other publications like Assaracus, Educe, THEM, Adrienne, Gertrude, *and* Chelsea Station, *in performing this role.*

Q: What is the poet's place in the world?

Poets have a really special role in our culture: to express—as well as language can—the difficult emotional challenges of being human: joy, grief, love, anger, lust, pride. When I turn to poetry, either as a writer or reader, I experience my humanity and access the language and knowledge I need to survive.

AUBADE

I dial The Number, punch a code
        to enter the backroom,
where I create a profile,
        with a deeper voice & the curt
monosyllables of attraction:
        Cut, thick, top, hot, now.

Nothing seems more hopeless
        than phone sex on Sunday morning,
early, around 5 or 6 AM, when the phone lines
        are crowded with club boys
tweaking home & middle-aged men
        waking stiff & hungry & alone.

Outside the empty streets shine still
        with lamplight & dew,
though in the city, it must be something
        else—gutter water
spreading its stain under the slow
        sizzle of random taxis.

As each man describes himself,
        this must be like the early,
golden days of radio,
        when voices were visceral,
each imagination shaping a different world,
        more real than its listener.

I come here to connect,
          if not in person,
then to needs that require anonymity.
          At twenty, I needed to know
I could be loved. At forty, I need
          to know I can be wanted.

I don't last long, shuffling the profiles
          like a deck of cards,
that spills, when gripped too tightly,
          to the floor, where a boy
crouches against a PHILCO, its voices
          beating against his heart.

ODE

It was what I wanted most:
            a hairy chest, like my father's,
like this senior's at school, poking
            through the mesh of his football jersey.
I'd watch him strut across the field, a 17-year-old god with olive skin,
            darkness threading his legs and forearms.
I wanted to curl up among his curls and sleep there,
            nestled in and breathing in the dank sweat at the roots.
  In 4th grade, I caught a friend scratching his groin,
            and at my look of wonder, he confided,
"It itches, don't you have any?"
            I felt left behind, especially when an aunt
would tease me about my *girl legs*, smooth until junior high,
            before sprouting light brown curls,
like commas scattered across the blank text of my skin.
            I wanted more.
I was learning the story of the body,
            showering with classmates, sneaking peeks
at the secrets their bodies would tell me.
            Once, I returned to my locker to find Ricky,
a senior, unstoppable on the soccer field,
            drying off, steaming in the fluorescent light.
It was winter, the gym's windows
            opaque and darkening by five o'clock,
and it was his hair, light golden brown all over
            his ruddy body, that glistened and transfixed me,
a boy trying to impress an older boy
            with talk of soccer practice.
When his towel fell away to reveal the mass of wiry curls
            around his small, bald cock,
I turned away, unable, finally,
            to pretend indifference any longer.

I dressed, then went home like any other night.
    But I knew then: it made you a man,
the smoothness of boyhood giving way to texture,
        a rough surface to kiss—other boys talked
of a girl's softness, but I wanted erosion:
    to be worn away by another boy's body.
Years later, I would wake in an empty bed,
    or beside a stranger, longing for the burn
of an unshaved face against my own,
    betrayed by my soft chest,
a man without the body of a man.
    Tucked into my baby book,
an envelope holds the remnants of my first haircut,
    a passage I don't remember,
but I cried, I am told, like most boys,
    before a trio of barbers,
whose shop buzzed with clippers, as men drowsed
        through fishing and hunting magazines,
or watched a football game on the fuzzy black and white set,
    perched on top of a soda machine.
Behold the mystery of manhood,
    as the clipper's electric teeth graze my neck,
the barber's swift scissors hovering
    over my head, nipping my ears,
a halo of blades,
    while my father whispers,
be a big boy, my mother holding
    a white envelope in her hands
to catch the first curls
    falling to the floor.

WHAT BRINGS ME BACK

These last days of winter, even light teases,
    coaxes me to an idle coffee outside a café,
where I watch college boys parade new bermudas,
    their legs pale and awkward in the day's final blush.
In high school, I wanted to impress a boy
    who wore his father's cotton shirts,
wrinkled and billowing from his thin waist.
    One night, on his front lawn, we chased
tequila with beer until we sank back into new grass,
    our throats open to the slick, cool burn,
tongues stung by salt, lips wet with lime—
    how clean desire felt then, like the air itself.
Last week, with dreams of T-shirts and crewcuts,
    I danced for hours, my body all light—
later, humming and alone in damp clothes, I drove
    for miles through vacant streets,
through steam plumes and flashing amber.

My skin pale and greasy, I wondered
if they dusted my body, whose prints would they find,
        what patterns? Last spring, another
boy's love bloomed to a raw *no*. Reeling
        in the clear June light, I wandered
Manhattan, his face everywhere—a half-smile
        between closing subway doors,
a street vendor's blunt, olive nose—until I collapsed
        in the Met before a nude of black granite.
Beneath a skylight's thin wash, I rocked on a bench,
        weeping at the sight of her back bending
to embrace her own knees, her head lowered
        as if she knew my shame, over the boy,
over this nameless grief each time another leaves,
        another layer, like ash, sheathing
this body alone. What brings me back
        can be thin as smoke clinging
to the arms of a dancer, or careless as the grace
        of workmen, or insistent as dawn
filling early crocuses, pale lanterns above cold mud.

SIP

Cold tin can against my boy lips,
I look into my father's grin and taste his Schlitz.
My mother's frying chicken in the kitchen behind us,
I can smell the grease and fat crackling in the air,
but then the foam reaches my tongue: a fizzy wave
of what's to come, salty and golden, a cold ache
that fills and fools my throat. He's holding the silver can
up to my lips because it's slippery and because both my hands
can't hold the whole thing, and he's got this look
on his face like I'm the best boy
he's ever seen and I want to smell like him, sweaty from work,
his hair still slick with Vitalis, a tired, day-long musk
rising from his body. When I start to choke,
he pulls the can away and wipes my mouth with his thumb,
raising a finger to his lips and winking, our secret.

REGRET

Midsummer, mild night, I'm walking Luella,
    when she sniffs a yellow silk tie left in a driveway.
Was it dropped from a laundry basket
    hurried from the car; no, you don't wash silk that way.
Perhaps the trace of this morning's garage sale?
    Picked-over, tied, brandished in a mirror, untied,
        picked back up,
Tied again, different neck, better knot, cast aside.
    Maybe a drunken husband, post-coital, coming
home late, trying to be quiet, the tie will be the final clue for the wife
    to discover or deny. Will the dew wash away the jasmine
        perfume & damp kisses?
Or fallen from the arms of a widow, who has finally boxed
    her husband's clothes,
    taken them away, out of sight, only to see this remnant of him
staring at her in tomorrow's bald light.

Whatever brought it here was a mistake.
    Whatever removes it will be a mystery.
Luella looks up, done sniffing and tugs her leash lightly
    to pull me back into this world, where a silk glyph
has made me pause & wonder what I have left behind.

DEAN

On a dirt road bordering a field
     behind his house,
I stood for a whole roll of black-&-white,
     not the poses of childhood,
but standing alone, against a backdrop
     of waist-high grass & budding trees.
He told me where to stand, but nothing else.
     My arms empty & awkward,
I didn't know whether to grin or frown,
     so I did both, folding my arms,
then releasing them, before fanning them out
     from behind my head, as after sex.
It was Sunday & the May heat was rising,
     my legs sore & sweaty
from hours of dancing the night before.
     A photographer who wore black,
he danced with his hips & his fists,
     his face a grimace
until asked his name. At four AM,
     we walked past houses
of folks dreaming of work & church,
     to the slow negotiation
of the front door & first kiss.
     I was drunk & afraid of my body,
his cock wet in my hands,
     a cry opening into water.

I never saw his pictures of me, yet each day
     I pass faces my age then,
with the same squint & flutter in their eyes,
     as they move toward what they want.
And their hearts, I imagine, are pure.
     I want to tell them
about losing something before you have it,
     or even know what it is.
But I hurry past them, toward home,
     as if somebody were waiting
for me to open the door & embrace him,
     or the idea of him.
And I think of Dean,
     our break up after a week
spent memorizing each other's bodies.
     Before spring arrives with its azaleas,
leaving me reckless for days with their color & light,
     I dip into a well of memory
for this first lover: his red, thinning hair,
     the white ridges of his back,
his wrist circling the lens, my face a blur,
     then distinct & his.

BEAUTIMOUS

When she talked fast,
    which was often,
my mother merged words,
    a lexicon of her own
for when language failed her,
    when the words she knew
could not contain
    what she had to say.
My favorite was *flusterated*,
    a mix of flustered & frustrated,
she would use most often
    around my father.
Another was *beautimous*,
    meaning beautiful & glamorous,
most often applied to herself,
    as she applied her makeup
in the morning, or when she watered
    her African violets
that crowned her kitchen window sill.
    I never corrected her.
And now I find these words
    surfacing in my mouth:
flusterated, I ride the tired subway,
    on the lookout for her face
in the passing crowd,
    vanishing & beautimous.

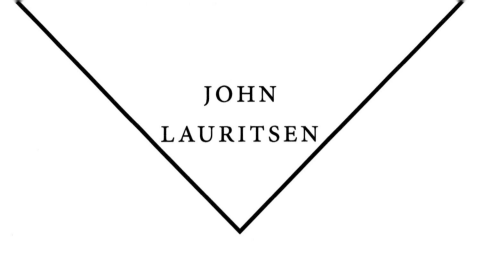

JOHN LAURITSEN

PAGAN PRESS

JOHN LAURITSEN, Harvard AB 1963, is a retired market research analyst. Lauritsen has been active in gay liberation since the summer of 1969 as a member of the New York Gay Liberation Front, Gay Activists Alliance, Gay Academic Union, and Columbia University Seminar on Homosexualities. He has twelve books to his credit. His writings have been widely published and translated. He now lives in Dorchester, Massachusetts.

Q: What is the publisher's greatest responsibility?

To publish well produced works, attractive and durable, which are engaging and truthful. To respect the rights of others: scholars, writers, artists, and other publishers. To have the courage of one's convictions. If I've taken my share of hard knocks, for telling the truth as I see it, I'm emboldened by the lines of Shelley:

> *To suffer woes which Hope thinks infinite;*
> *To forgive wrongs darker than death or night;*
> *To defy Power, which seems omnipotent;*
> *To love, and bear; to hope till Hope creates*
> *From its own wreck the thing it contemplates;*
> *Neither to change, nor falter, nor repent;*
> *This, like thy glory, Titan, is to be*
> *Good, great and joyous, beautiful and free;*
> *This is alone Life, Joy, Empire, and Victory!*

Percy Bysshe Shelley, *Prometheus Unbound*

JOHN LAURITSEN

A HISTORY OF PAGAN PRESS

When I founded Pagan Press in 1982, I never imagined what I would be getting into: furious controversies and struggles where I would lay my life on the line. I intended to "publish books of interest to the intelligent gay man"—especially some of the great classics of male love, works that were virtually unknown then, even to those in the Homophile and Gay Liberation movements. Resisting the push to "inclusiveness" (LGBTQ . . . blippety-blip), I've remained faithful to my original mandate.

"Pagan" is an expression of gay Hellenism; it denotes the culture of Classical Antiquity, especially Ancient Greece, the cultural homeland of male love—the outlook before antigay superstition came to prevail in the 4th century AD. I agree with Nietzsche, who wrote: "The Greeks remain the foremost cultural phenomenon of history—they knew and they *did* what had to be done; Christianity, which despised the body, has so far been mankind's greatest calamity." (*Twilight of the Idols*, tr. JL)

The Pagan Press logo is a Victorian rendition of a Pompeiian fresco depicting Cupid in a chariot drawn by goats. This is a light-hearted representation of a famous and powerful symbol, the Charioteer in Plato's *Phaedrus*, one of his two dialogues on love. The drawing was used on the front cover of Edward Carpenter's book, *Angels' Wings*, embossed in gold against a dark blue background.

My first gay writings were done in 1970: pamphlets published by The Red Butterfly, the radical cell of the New York Gay Liberation Front (GLF). Although I wasn't the only writer, I prepared the mimeograph stencils and ran the mimeograph machine. We couldn't afford professional typesetting or offset printing. All the Red Butterfly pamphlets are now on my website. URLs are listed at the end of this article.

My first book, co-authored with David Thorstad, was *The Early Homosexual Rights Movement (1864-1935)* (TEHRM), published by Times Change Press in 1974. As short as our book was, not much over a hundred pages, it was based on thousands of pages of primary sources, mostly in German. It told the "early history of a movement generally thought not to have an early history." TEHRM was a small press best seller, going through many printings and two editions. It was translated into French, Italian, German, and Spanish, and has been one of the most referenced gay books since Stonewall.

As a self-publisher I advanced technologically from the mimeograph to offset. At Come! Unity Press, a quasi-anarchist collective on 17th Street in New York City, I learned how to run an A.B. Dick offset press, make plates, and do folding and binding. For typesetting I used electric typewriters, the best being a proportionately spaced IBM Executive. Here I produced leaflets and booklets, the most ambitious being *Religious Roots of the Taboo on Homosexuality: A Materialist View* (1974), which is now online. Come! Unity Press insisted that everything printed there be free to anyone who could not afford the cover price, which for *Religious Roots* was 75¢. Although never advertised or distributed commercially, several thousand copies were sold, and it was translated into German. *Religious Roots* was superseded by my 1998 book, *A Freethinker's Primer of Male Love*, about which there is more below.

At Come! Unity Press I also wrote and published a pamphlet for the Gay Activists Alliance, *Repeal The New York Consensual Sodomy Statute!* (1974). The GAA Political Action Committee gave a copy of this pamphlet to every member of the New York State Legislature— which did indeed repeal the Consensual Sodomy Statute, years before the U.S. Supreme Court struck down all remaining state sodomy statutes. I'd like to think my little pamphlet (now online) deserves some of the credit.

Now I'm getting to Pagan Press. For years I had been rummaging through used bookstores, in city after city, looking for books by Edward Carpenter, John Addington Symonds, Magnus Hirschfeld, and other forerunners of Gay Liberation. I was especially fond of Carpenter's *Ioläus: An Anthology of Friendship*. First published in 1902, *Ioläus* had been out-of-print for over half a century when I chose it as the first Pagan Press title. With Dan Poynter's *Manual of Self-Publishing* as my guide, I obtained a business certificate, ISBNs, office supplies, etc., and started making camera-ready layouts. My book was a facsimile reproduction of an attractive American edition from 1917, with photos taken from Carpenter's autobiography, *My Days and Dreams*. The printer did a good job, and the end result was attractive. *Ioläus* was reviewed favorably in the gay press, and was selected by Richard Hall in *The Advocate* as one of the ten best gay books for 1982. It quickly sold out.

When I was a freshman at Harvard, I read two works which transformed the shame of my adolescence into self-acceptance: Plato's *Symposium* and John Addington Symonds's *A Problem in Greek Ethics*. Scales fell from my eyes as I learned that the Ancient Greeks, founders of Western Civilization, had accepted male love as a part of life and had granted it a place of honor. The Greek gods themselves had male lovers. As important as the Symonds essay was to me, I found that it was almost unknown, even to gay liberationists. The second Pagan Press book was a centennial edition (1883-1983): John Addington Symonds, *Male Love: A Problem in Greek Ethics and Other Writings*— which included all of *A Problem in Greek Ethics*, selected chapters from *A Problem in Modern Ethics* and *The Genius of Greek Art*, some letters from Symonds to Edward Carpenter, my own Introduction, and a Foreword by poet and Symonds scholar, Robert Peters. Richard Hall selected it as one of 1983's ten best. History Professor William A. Percy, one of the editors of the *Encyclopedia of Homosexuality*, said that reading my Symonds book changed his life and led him to become a gay activist and scholar.

Then the Gay Health Crisis struck. Tentatively at first, I got involved in a struggle which would define my life for decades. This is not the place for a long "AIDS" narrative; it's hard for me to discuss this without bitterness, and I'd much rather discuss poetry. Briefly, I'm an AIDS critic or dissident, someone who rejects the prevailing AIDS paradigm. A 2010 talk I gave in Vienna—"The 'AIDS' Hoax and Gay Men"—summarizes my views and is online.

In 1983 I began studying the medical literature on "AIDS," which then consisted of about two dozen articles. In those early years various hypotheses were advanced as to the nature and causes of the new syndrome (still unnamed), including toxicology. Since I was both a professional survey research analyst and a gay scholar, I imagined that I could help out the government investigators, who seemed to be foundering. How naive I was! It soon became apparent that the government epidemiologists were not just incompetent, but dishonest. It was obvious, even then, that AIDS was not behaving like an infectious disease, but was rigidly compartmentalized, confined almost entirely to two main risk groups: heroin users and gay men. Serious investigation ought to have been done regarding non-infectious health risks in these two groups—but the government "scientists" were hell-bent on promoting a novel infectious agent as the sole cause.

In the fall of 1981, Hank Wilson, a long-time gay activist in San Francisco, founded the Committee to Monitor Poppers. He began acquiring a large collection of medical and other reports on the nitrite inhalants, corresponding with researchers and public officials, and warning about the dangers of the premier gay drug. My friend Arthur Evans, whom I'd known from GLF and GAA in New York, wrote an article, "Poppers: An ugly side of gay business" (*Coming Up!*, San Francisco, November 1981). For their efforts, Hank and Arthur were denounced as "gay traitors." *The Advocate*, which received many tens of thousands of dollars in poppers advertising, refused to publish information critical of poppers, whether from Hank or from scientists.

The original poppers were a pharmaceutical drug, amyl nitrite, enclosed in little glass ampules which were "popped" under the nose. These were used by the elderly for emergency relief of heart pain. In contrast, the poppers used by gay men were combinations of butyl nitrite, isobutyl nitrite, and other chemicals, enclosed in little bottles. Some gay men would binge on poppers over the weekend; some snorted them all day long; some needed them as a sexual crutch, without which they no longer could have sex, even solitary masturbation.

Poppers are hazardous to the health in many different ways: They damage the immune system and lungs. They can cause anemia severe enough to cause death within minutes. Poppers are strongly mutagenic and have the potential to cause cancer by producing deadly N-nitroso compounds. Poppers can cause death or brain damage from cardiovascular collapse or stroke. At present, poppers represent the only tenable hypothesis for the occurrence of Kaposi's sarcoma in gay men.

I started collaborating with Hank in 1983. A few hours after the first time I spoke out publicly on poppers, the phone rang—a woman's voice, cold and professional: "Don't be surprised if you don't wake up in the morning [CLICK]." It was my first death threat, and I took it seriously. I made sure that the iron gates on the windows were closed and the door securely locked; then I spent a sleepless night. The next day I called Hank, who also had received death threats. We decided that the best way to protect ourselves was to be as public as possible, to gain allies and make sure the mob would have more to lose than gain by killing us. I am still alive; Hank died several years ago from lung cancer.

Hank and I published a pamphlet on the dangers of poppers, and whenever given an opportunity we published articles in the gay press. In 1986 we co-authored the third Pagan Press book, *Death Rush: Poppers & AIDS, With annotated bibliography*. Technology had advanced: I now had an Alcatel PC, superior to the original IBM PC, and an early version of WordPerfect. No more mimeograph stencils or typewriters or white-out liquid. Since laser printers of the time were poor quality, and dot matrix printers even worse, I did typesetting with a Qume daisy-wheel printer: a proportionately spaced typeface based on Herman Zapf's Optima. Ian Young's partner, Wulf, designed the cover: a surrealistic rendering of a poppers bottle with a skull & crossbones. Between sales and the dozens we gave out, copies of our little book (64 pages) were soon gone. It is online.

In February 1985 my first major AIDS article, "CDC's Tables Obscure AIDS-Drugs Connection," was published in the *Philadelphia Gay News*. Also in 1985 two AIDS articles of mine were published in the *New York Native*, which in the next eleven years would publish over fifty of my articles. The *Native* was then the foremost gay publication, sold on newsstands all over the world.

In 1987 I became the first journalist to interview Peter Duesberg, Professor of Molecular Biology, who had shown that HIV, the so-called "AIDS virus," could not possibly be the cause of the syndrome, or even be harmful (*Cancer Research*, March 1987). Also in 1987 I became a leading critic of the drug AZT, using FDA documents obtained under the Freedom of Information Act to show that AZT had been approved for marketing on the basis of fraudulent research.

The fourth Pagan Press book, *Poison By Prescription: The AZT Story*, was published in 1990. It had a Foreword by Peter Duesberg and consisted mostly of my AZT articles from the *New York Native*. Like *Death Rush* it was produced using my PC, WordPerfect, and the Qume daisy-wheel printer. I was afraid of being sued for libel by Burroughs Wellcome, the manufacturer of AZT, so I made sure that all statements in the book would stand up in a court of law. They didn't sue. *Poison By Prescription* sold out four printings and provided income that was welcome, since I was now trying to make my living as a writer. It is now online as a facsimile PDF book.

The fifth Pagan Press book, *The AIDS War: Propaganda, Profiteering and Genocide from the Medical-Industrial Complex*, was published in 1993. This is a big book: 480 pages and weighing 1.5 pounds. It has 35 chapters, 4 excursus (or digressions), and 28 illustrations. By this time laser printers could do acceptable typesetting—I used a 386 PC and an HP Laserjet III printer: Garamond Antiqua for text, Univers for tables, and Shannon for the front cover and spine. WordPerfect 5.1 for DOS, which I still use for all my serious writing, has a powerful indexing feature, which enabled me to make separate indices of names and subjects. *The AIDS War* sold well and is still in print; less than a hundred copies are still left out of the fourth printing.

In 1995 I became a year-round resident of Provincetown. My first Pagan Press book from P-town, number six, was *The AIDS Cult: Essays on the gay health crisis* (1997), edited by Ian Young and myself. Ian wrote the following for the back cover:

> What really causes AIDS? A virus from Africa? Or our own neglect—or worse—of whole categories of our population?
>
> The essays in *The AIDS Cult* show how a number of different beliefs, group interests and social forces conspire to make us "sick."
>
> With varied backgrounds and different vantage points, the eight contributors offer a fresh, radical view of our society's health crisis, as manifested in the gay community. They challenge us to reexamine our assumptions about AIDS and terminate the mass sacrificial ritual we have been enacting.

By now I had a 486 PC and a software program that allowed me to use Adobe postscript typefaces: Giovanni Mardersteig's Dante for the text and Plantin for the front cover. *The AIDS Cult* is still in print.

My next book from P-town, *A Freethinker's Primer of Male Love* (1987), Pagan Press number seven, had simmered on the back burner for well over a decade. It took me that long to write a book that short, only 96 pages. Written in an aphoristic style, it was then and is now the only work to champion Gay Liberation from an explicitly secular humanist standpoint, one openly hostile to the Abrahamic religions. The opening paragraph:

> This is the story of how a form of love, highly esteemed in Classical Antiquity, fell under a religious taboo — how as a result its practitioners suffered dishonor, imprisonment, torture, and death. It is about a crippling of the male psyche through the twin forces of superstition and tyranny.

A Freethinker's Primer is still in print.

And now I return to my first love, English literature and poetry. Some time in the 1970's, doing research in the New York 42nd Street Library, I came across a catalog entry for a translation of Plato's *Symposium* by Percy Bysshe Shelley (1792-1822). Intrigued, I got access to the rare books collection and began reading it. A rare book indeed, it was one of only 100 copies that had been "printed for private circulation" in 1931; it was the first time Shelley's translation, done in 1818, had ever been published unbowdlerized and complete. I was spellbound. Book and print seemed to vanish as I heard the voices of friends discussing Love with each other, men who had died 24 centuries ago. The next day I returned with camera and copy stand to photograph the book. (The rare books division allowed this, but not photocopying.)

If Shelley's *Banquet* had been published when completed, it would have been the first in English to present the genders correctly, making it clear that the dialogue concerned male love. Shelley's introductory essay—"A Discourse on the Manners of the Antient [*sic*] Greeks Relative to the Subject of Love"—would have been the first in English to discuss sex between males. But the time was not ripe for publication: during Shelley's entire lifetime, men and boys in England were hanged for making love to each other; the ideas of Plato and the customs of Ancient Greece could not be mentioned. Shelley's widow, Mary, first suppressed both translation and essay, and then, nineteen years after Shelley's death, published them in a drastically bowdlerized form, in which whole sections were cut out, *love* was changed to *friendship*, *men* to *human beings*, and so on.

Ever since founding Pagan Press I had intended to publish Shelley's *Symposium*, which he titled *The Banquet*, but never got around to it until 2001, when it became the eighth Pagan Press book and the second published in P-town.

Shelley's translation towers above all others because it is *alive*. He had a superb gift for dialogue, as evident in his poems and novels: even when speakers indulge in grand rhetoric, their words are fluent and natural. Shelley does justice to Plato's ideas, which are expressed clearly and cogently, but he also conveys the wit, irony, and feeling of the original—and there are passages of beautiful prose-poetry, especially in the speech of Alcibiades the Beautiful, the dramatic climax of the dialogue. The Pagan Press *Banquet* has been assigned in literature classes; it has sold well and is still in print.

I got to know Shelley well, reading everything I could find by or about him, especially the writings of people who had known him well. I came to the conclusion that all of the men in the Shelley-Byron circle in Italy were at least bisexual—notwithstanding their various wives and mistresses—and wrote an article, "Was Percy Bysshe Shelley Gay?", which was published in the electronic *Gay Today*. In 2002 I delivered a paper, "Male Love in the Shelley-Byron Circle" to a group of gay scholars in New York City. In 2003 I moved from P-town to Dorchester (part of Boston), where I live now.

When I re-read *Frankenstein* in the original, unbowdlerized 1818 edition, I came across examples of homoeroticism, both obvious and coded, and passages unmistakably representing Shelley's life, ideas and prose style. Further research convinced me that *Frankenstein* is Shelley's work, his and his alone, despite the orthodox belief that it was written by his second wife, Mary. I was warned to expect a backlash if I debunked Mary's authorship, but went on to publish the ninth Pagan Press book, *The Man Who Wrote Frankenstein* (TMWWF). By now I had a 1200 dpi laser printer, which can do excellent typesetting. I used Eric Gill's typeface, Joanna, which is plain but distinctive, and superbly readable. Following Gill's advice ("The Procrustean Bed," *An Essay on Typography*), I did *not* justify the right-hand margins.

The Man Who Wrote Frankenstein received some excellent pre-publication publicity: a news story in the *Sunday Times* (London) and a rave review by Camille Paglia in *Salon.com*, which concluded:

> This is a funny, wonderful, revelatory book that I hope will inspire ambitious graduate students and young faculty to

strike blows for truth in our mired profession, paralyzed by convention and fear.

Thanks to the publicity, *The Man Who Wrote Frankenstein* sold well over a hundred copies before its official publication date. But Furies had been unleashed. All over the Internet, bloggers, none of whom would read my book, called me a homosexual, a misogynist, a fascist, a bully, a geek, and a schlub. I learned that not only is Mary Shelley's authorship of *Frankenstein* sacred dogma, but many of the top specialists in English Romanticism are heavily invested in the myth that she was a writer of genius and the author of *Frankenstein*. I became a pariah. Senior professors closed ranks against me, and junior faculty, with few exceptions, followed their lead.

The Man Who Wrote Frankenstein has three theses: 1) Frankenstein is a great work, which has consistently been underrated and misinterpreted; 2) The real author of *Frankenstein* is Percy Bysshe Shelley; and 3) male love is a central theme. Most of TMWWF is devoted to the first and third, which I consider the most important. Although I provide ample proof for the second thesis, it is really obvious, once the authorship question is broached; the tenacious belief in Mary's authorship is interesting mainly as psychology—which could also be said about belief in Santa Claus. Not all of my readers agreed that *Frankenstein* was a great work, or that male love was a central theme, but virtually all were convinced that Mary Shelley could not be the author.

The Man Who Wrote Frankenstein was reviewed favorably by gay reviewers, especially those with a love of Shelley; it was reviewed viciously by straight reviewers with ties to Academia. The latter didn't bother coming to grips with my arguments, but relied on misrepresentation, insults, and *ad hominem* attacks.

The Chronicle Review published a letter of mine, which concluded: "*Frankenstein* is a radical, disturbing, poetically powerful work. It is fully worthy of its true author, Shelley, one of the greatest poets in English."

I am especially proud of the last two Pagan Press books, which are translations of Aeschylus plays, done by Shelley and his cousin, Thomas Medwin. These are not really gay books, although the dramatist (Aeschylus), the translators (Shelley and Medwin), the editor (me), and other authors included (Goethe, John Addington Symonds) are no strangers to male love. I was led to these translations by reading Ernest J. Lovell, Jr.'s biography, *Captain Medwin: Friend of Byron and Shelley* (1962), which described Medwin as "one of the most outrageously misrepresented men in all literary history." (Hint: Mary Shelley and he didn't like each other.) Lovell bestows high praise on six Aeschylus translations that were published in *Fraser's Magazine* under Medwin's name in the 1830's, and gives long quotations from the *Agamemnon* translation. I was struck by the power and beauty of the translation excerpts, and knew that I would have to read the translations in their entirety. Widener Library, one of the world's great research libraries, did not have copies of *Fraser's*, but the New York 42nd Street library did, so I made a special trip to New York City to photocopy them. Then, during the long, cold isolation of a Provincetown winter, I typed them. This was hard work, since the type was small and the photocopy quality was poor (the *Fraser's* originals were brittle and had darkened with age).

Even as I typed I realized that these forgotten translations were masterpieces of English poetry. Gradually I realized that Shelley was, at the very least, a collaborator with Medwin—and this was confirmed by biographical evidence.

The tenth Pagan Press book is the Medwin-Shelley translation of the *Oresteia*, the only extant trilogy in Greek drama. The first play of the trilogy, *Agamemnon*, is widely considered one of the supreme masterpieces of world literature. I agree, and while I may be a minority of one, now consider the Medwin-Shelley translation of the *Oresteia* to be the greatest play in the English language. Shelley's hand is apparent in the dialogue passages, rendered into pentameter blank verse, and especially in the choral passages, rendered into traditional as well as intricately original verse forms—and Shelley was the master of more verse forms than any other poet in English. Almost two centuries after it was composed, the Medwin-Shelley translation of the *Oresteia* is still unequalled for dramatic power and poetry. It could effectively be put on the stage.

Oresteia was the first Pagan Press book to use digital printing, which has greatly changed both the techniques of production and the economics of print runs. Whereas in offset I submitted camera-ready copy to the printer, in digital I prepared a PDF file with fully embedded fonts, which I simply sent to the printer via e-mail. Again I used the Joanna typeface, which was perfect for the play: it is readable, but also, large and with generous leading, it encourages the reader to read the lines slowly enough that he hears them. When printing a book by offset, it makes no sense to do fewer than 1,000 copies, since the cost is only a little more than doing 500—and doing 2,000 doesn't cost that much more than doing 1,000. Digital is a whole new ball game: there is an initial setup charge, but after that the cost is simply so much per copy, regardless of how many. This means that by digital it makes sense to print 50 copies or even fewer; if reprints are needed, the cost is again only so much per copy (plus shipping).

The eleventh Pagan Press book is the Medwin-Shelley translation of the Aeschylus play, *Prometheus Bound*, together with Shelley's own play, *Prometheus Unbound*, generally considered his masterpiece, as well as an appreciation by John Addington Symonds and my own translation of Goethe's poem, *Prometheus*. Shelley had been working on a *Prometheus Bound* translation for years, engrossed by the theme of rebellion against tyranny. A comparison of the translation with Shelley's own play shows unmistakably that he was the primary craftsman of the former. The Pagan Press *Prometheus* is a companion of *Oresteia*; the same production techniques and typeface were used.

Prometheus is selling well, perhaps because of the sexy cover painting by Jean-Louis-Cesar Lair, depicting Prometheus as a beautiful, naked youth, bound by chains and with a vulture pecking at his liver. Lair finished the painting in 1819, the same year that Shelley finished *Prometheus Unbound*. Already the Pagan Press *Prometheus* has been assigned in a college literature course.

That is a history of Pagan Press. All of the titles have at least broken even, and a couple have been best sellers by the standards of serious, non-fiction, small press books. They are described in the online Booklist below. If ordered through me, I'll give substantial discounts for *Assaracus* readers—just contact me via e-mail, and I'll send information. Payment can be made easily and securely by PayPal.

Since *Assaracus* is a poetry journal, I'll add that from time to time I translate poetry or write some of my own. My first chapbook, *Poems & Translations* (Come! Unity Press, 1975), had translations of poems by Stefan George, Bertolt Brecht, and Hölderlin, with German and English on facing pages, along with a few poems of my own.

Then, under the Pagan Press imprint, and thinking small, I did two copy machine chapbooks. I developed the techniques whereby I could publish them using nothing but my PC, WordPerfect 6.2 for DOS, laser printer, and copy machine. The first, *Backburner Poems*, again had translations and my own poems. The last one, to which I whimsically assigned an ISBN, was only three sheets of paper, folded: *Hölderlin Poems, translated by John Lauritsen* (2013)—English translation and German original on facing pages. Like his older German contemporaries—Friedrich Schiller and Johann Wolfgang Goethe—Johann Christian Friedrich Hölderlin was a fervent Hellenist, but he went beyond them. To Hölderlin the Greeks gods were still alive, and he worshipped them. Here are my translations of two poems, which suggest that Hölderlin was a devotee of Greek Love:

TO THE SUN GOD

Where art thou? My soul grows dark, drunk
From all thy joy; for I have just seen,
Weary from his journey,
The ravishing god-youth

Bathe his young locks in golden clouds;
And my unwilling eyes follow him;
Though he's gone far away
To faithful people who revere him still.

I love you, Earth! For you must mourn with me!
And our mourning, like childhood pain,
Turns into slumber, just as the wind
Rustles and whispers through lyre-strings

Until the Master's finger draws
A fairer tone, so mist and dreams
Around us play, till the lover returns and
Kindles life and spirit within.

Friedrich Hölderlin, tr. John Lauritsen

SOCRATES AND ALCIBIADES

"Why do you humble yourself, Holy Socrates,
"To this youth all the time? Know you nothing greater?
     "Why do your eyes look lovingly,
     "As though on gods, on him?"

He whose thoughts run deepest, loves the liveliest,
Noble youth understands, he who's looked into the world,
     And the wise in the end
     Often bow down to the beautiful.

Friedrich Hölderlin, tr. John Lauritsen

URLs (all are case sensitive)

Pagan Press Booklist:
http://paganpressbooks.com/BOOKLIST.HTM

Red Butterfly section of my personal website:
http://paganpressbooks.com/jpl/TRB.HTM

Religious Roots of the Taboo on Homosexuality:
http://paganpressbooks.com/jpl/RELROOTS.PDF

"Repeal the New York Consensual Sodomy Statute!":
http://paganpressbooks.com/jpl/REPEAL.HTM

"The 'AIDS' Hoax and Gay Men":
http://paganpressbooks.com/jpl/VIENNA.HTM

Arthur Evans, "Poppers: An ugly side of gay business":
http://paganpressbooks.com/jpl/EVANSPOP.HTM

Death Rush: Poppers & AIDS:
http://paganpressbooks.com/jpl/POPBOOK.HTM

Poison By Prescription: The AZT Story:
http://paganpressbooks.com/jpl/POISON.PDF

Camille Paglia's review of TMWWF:
http://paganpressbooks.com/jpl/PAGLIA.HTM

E-mail: john.lauritsen@verizon.net

Personal website: paganpressbooks.com/jpl

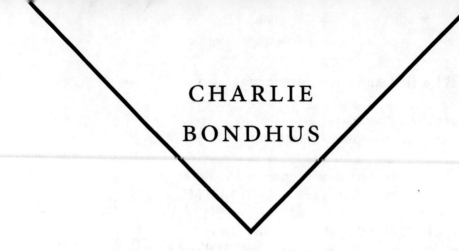

CHARLIE BONDHUS

THE GOOD MEN PROJECT

CHARLIE BONDHUS is the author of *All the Heat We Could Carry*, winner of the 2013 Main Street Rag Poetry Book Award, and poetry editor at *The Good Men Project*. His previous books include *What We Have Learned to Love*, which won Brickhouse Books' 2008-2009 Stonewall Competition, and *How the Boy Might See It* (Pecan Grove Press, 2009) which was a finalist for the 2007 Blue Light Press First Book Award. He has also published a gayish novella, *Monsters and Victims* (Gothic Press, 2010). He holds an MFA in creative writing from Goddard College and a Ph.D. in literature from the University of Massachusetts, Amherst. He teaches at Raritan Valley Community College in New Jersey.

Q: Who, writing now, excites you?

Many poets writing now excite me. Everyone I publish at The Good Men Project *excites me. I will name Dwight Allen Gray as one in particular since his book* Overwatch, *which is about his experiences serving in Iraq, helped me to write my own* All the Heat We Could Carry. *Beyond that, I feel like I'd have to list every poet I've published on GMP! So instead, here's a link to our archive: http://goodmenproject.com/category/poetry-2/*

A FEW GOOD MEN

I was more than happy to accept the opportunity to helm *The Good Men Project*'s (goodmenproject.com) poetry section when it was offered to me in November 2013 partly because I want to support and promote poetry, and partly because I've long been interested in questions of masculinity. Many magazines, blogs, journals, and websites are dedicated to women's issues—and I think this is important because women have been and continue to be marginalized—yet I believe it's also important to look closely at men and masculinity, lest we fall into the destructive assumption that men are somehow the "default" gender. Besides, I think men also struggle with gender issues—though we don't hear about it as much because guys are supposed to be "stoic."

I think that questions of what it means to be a man are highly relevant to gay/bisexual men, as so many of us have had our manhood invalidated at one point or another in our lives. Yet homosexuality does not preclude masculinity. On the contrary, I think that, as men who love men, we have a unique view on and appreciation of manhood. While there's the obvious angle—we frequently have a license and a leeway that heterosexual men often don't to explore alternate expressions of masculinity—I also think that gay/bisexual men, as inhabiters of male bodies/minds and lovers of male bodies/minds, have an important perspective on masculinity. In other words, as individuals who've been emasculated by our society, yet whose sexual and affectional orientation is directed towards men, many of us tend to think about our masculinity in a way heterosexual men may not need to.

As the poetry editor of *The Good Men Project*, I hope to empower gay and bisexual men to speak on an even keel with their heterosexual brothers, to give voice both to their unique concerns, and to establish dialogues with heterosexual men. In so doing, it's my hope that we as gay/bisexual men can build a greater kinship with heterosexual men and that, together, men of all identities can promote healthier, more productive, and more creative models of masculinity.

CATHOLIC BOY

The boy next door takes out his
pocketknife, slits his palm along the fate line,
says "we can be blood
brothers now," hands kissing wetly

       as we stand in the empty
       canal behind my house, where last summer
       we built forts out of sticks
       and mud, worshipping God in our own way,

as my mother put it, every act
done faithfully an act of prayer, even sex,
which isn't queer
as long as we don't touch, two boys

       side-by-side, jeans and underwear crumpled around
       socks and shoes, colonnades of cypress arching above.
       In church I wear a necktie and a powder-blue
       Oxford shirt, polished black shoes that carry me next

door to the working class high school
of chain-link and cigarette butts, broken
windows, Friday fish, mass, and confession.
What the nuns don't know is dog hot

       Sunday afternoons, when I travel over highways
       to rest stops and kneel on a tiled floor
       to take in what I lack; a man placing his hands on my
       head and saying "easy now,

go as slow as you need to." I tilt my head back
and the bread-thin body of Christ
is tasteless as candle wax, stiff as my knees
from kneeling beside my mother

      in an empty chapel, beneath my savior's
      naked limbs, praying for a cure,
      or, if there isn't one, at least a bold
      Semitic brow, a chin prominent

even when bowed, pecs and arms
that crunch and flex
beneath the lash, and a set of abs
fit for a crucifixion.

MEMORIAL DAY BARBECUE

People screamed. Burgers and dogs hissed themselves
brown. Beer bottles spat foam. More than a few of us
were drunk.

He looked better than I'd expected. I was picturing
more—how should I say this?—draggled. Wild-eyed.
Like a prophet who's seen hell.

He laughed with everyone, like nothing had changed.
Maybe war, like anything else, is something you get
over.

We noticed when he disappeared. I was chatting with
his partner, who didn't say anything about it. We
watched a crow assault a piece of bread.

I didn't want to embarrass anybody, but I was curious.
I walked around the house, past the red-streaked
zinnias, and out to the street. He was sitting in the
passenger seat of their car.

He wasn't reading a magazine or making a call. He
was just sitting, with his hands on his knees, the trees'
shadows passing over his face like large insects.

Did he carry a gun in the glove compartment?

I was remembering every Vietnam movie I'd ever seen,

his eyes two unpinned grenades, overturned tables and
smashed chairs, bowls of finger food shattered into
small universes.

When he saw me, I felt like I'd been caught stealing.
We stared at each other for a few seconds before he
smiled and raised his hand. He got out of the car and
walked over to me. He lit a cigarette as we talked
about this party and past ones, people we knew who
weren't here, the summer heat's early arrival.

I saw the glass edges of the moment. Everything
breakable: the pavement, the flowers, the silent car, all
of it.

I turned to walk back. He caught my arm.

"If they ask, tell them I was in the bathroom."

A QUIET DAY IN KANDAHAR

Twenty-nine days since we saw action,
a skirmish by the ridge
which left eight dead.

Gonzalez takes out the naked lady cards
and asks if anyone wants to play.

The boys have named their favorites—
blonde Kelly, the queen of clubs; olive-skinned
Anya straddling five spades; Misty's thighs
cutting a trice of diamonds; all-American
Emily balancing a pair of hearts on her silicone jugs.

Gonzalez will die next week,
but for now he deals
shit hands to Patel and Mendoza,
who bluff and grin
like two enemies brandishing unloaded weapons.

I sit on a cooler and smoke,
watching the card game and listening
to the chirping bee-eaters in the tree above.

Today there is no cackling gunfire.
Nothing moves
on the horizon except a steppe eagle,
gliding on a heavy breeze which rolls into camp
and scatters the cards,
every which way, filling the air
with a flurry of tits and ass.

Laughing and cursing, we chase them,
leaving our rifles on the ground.

For the moment, I forget where I am

as I grasp cards by the handful,
filling my fists with suits of women.

Who could think about war
at a time like this,
when naked ladies are dancing
in the air?

We save all but Anya and Emily.

Two civilian casualties, Mendoza snickers,
dumping his cards on the table.

Dude. Not cool, says Patel,
biting back a smile.

Gonzalez makes a spitting/farting noise
with his lips and then busts into a belly laugh.

Mendoza joins in, then me,
and finally Patel,
the four of us laughing
at the flying cards,
at Mendoza's poor taste,

and then at something more,
something that sets fire
to our bone marrow.

The sun glares down
as the bee-eaters fly off
and the steppe eagle coasts over the horizon.

We laugh so hard that,
from a distance,
it must sound like screaming.

Last month, we killed eight people.

WHAT HE LEFT

I know it's broken,
but the cool, dark potential still unnerves me.

Many things are wrong:
something (the bullets?) rattling
like coins in a jar, the bright silver firing pin
snapped like a link in an old rosary.

Its black weight makes my hands
crinkle, two leaves flaking apart;
the only way I can hold a thing so potent
is with the knowledge that the moving parts
are immobilized.

It's always been this way,

loving chrome-cut men,
so solid there's not a hollow space to accommodate
the rising contractions of the heart.

You showed it to me one day,
explained hammers, pins, and primer;
cartridges and sparks, mechanical energy
and chemical reactions, you said

firing a gun is a little like writing fiction;
there's an initiating action,
a chain of events, the moment of crisis,
and then the falling tension,
the irrevocable resolution, but,

I know ours is not that kind of story.

No climax: you simply packed
what was useful and indisputably yours,
leaving me everything that might have been
ours, so why abandon this broken, deadly bit
of memory you carried
through Afghanistan?

Hard and cold as canteen water,
a memento of more than one desert,
I cradle it as though it were your heart.

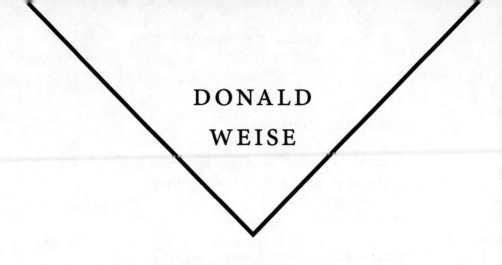

DONALD WEISE

MAGNUS BOOKS

DONALD WEISE, the editorial director of Magnus Books, has twenty years of publishing experience, the majority of which has been devoted to LGBT literature. He's served as Publisher of Alyson Books and Senior Editor at Carroll & Graf Publishers. Don was named by *Publishers Weekly* as an industry "Change Maker" and listed among *Out Magazine*'s "100 Most Intriguing Gay Men and Lesbians" of the year.

Q: What advice would you give an aspiring editor?

I never had any formal training as an editor, and it wasn't something I'd ever aspired to become. It beat answering the telephones at the time, so I decided to try it. You have to keep in mind that my path isn't typical and much of what I know and have done probably wouldn't apply to a newcomer at one of the big houses, where best sellers are all that matter. From my own experience, though, I'd say don't be afraid to approach the biggest names you know, including people in publishing who might help your career. Being gay has been a big asset to me in part because it broke down the publishing world into a community. There are only so many of us and sooner or later, at least here in New York, you begin to feel that you've met everyone. I've always loved helping new editors meet older people in influential positions that might help their careers because I got so little help when I was starting off. Basically, as it says in my essay, Gore Vidal gave me my break, so you could say I'm here thanks to him.

DONALD WEISE

TALKING SEX WITH GORE VIDAL

Recently we saw the publication of journalist Tim Teeman's biography *In Bed with Gore Vidal: Hustlers, Hollywood, and the Private World of an American Master.* As the subtitle suggests, the book for the first time looks at Vidal's romantic and sexual lives and their influence on his writing and political advocacy. I say "for the first time" because a book on this topic could not have been published before Vidal's death in August 2012; not only would he have sued the publisher, but his family members and closest friends, interviewed at length in the book, would not have spoken on record as they have— and with surprising openness—because they too would have incited Vidal's fury. Vidal spent a lifetime suing people, and I gather this only became more prevalent as the years passed. When asked late in life what replaces sex when one gets older, Vidal answered, "Litigation."

I've been a big fan of Vidal all my adult life. It wasn't so much that I loved the novels but that I was fascinated that a gay man (who never really came out as such—most of his literary peers didn't either) could be so erudite and clever and openly disdainful of so much and not only get away with it but be celebrated. In short he was the first gay man who showed me that you could live life on your own terms, at least if you had the talent and guts to pull it off.

Because of my tremendous admiration for Vidal, I wasn't sure when I commissioned the biography from Tim about a year ago whether I'd like the book—or Vidal—after reading it. As Tim shows us, the Vidal I knew—that anyone knew—was a public persona carefully constructed and maintained for years, since the end of World War II when he published his first novel and up to his death. His longevity was awesome, and if the legend allowed for that longevity, I personally didn't mind. But what then would I think of a book that looked beyond the legend, showing the Master for all of his flaws and vulnerabilities, perhaps even his own homophobia, for the first time?

Rather than answer this right away I'd like to speak instead to the book itself, because what Tim handed in was infinitely richer and more in-depth than anything we discussed in the beginning. For example, I hadn't anticipated that actress Claire Bloom would share with Tim the intimate details of her romantic friendship with Vidal, including rumors of Vidal having proposed marriage to her, or that his Hollywood pimp for decades (the inimitable Scotty Bowers) would catalog all the male movie stars Vidal had hooked up with. I wasn't expecting Vidal's half-sister (I wasn't even expecting a half-sister) to open up about the private side of his decades-long public feud with William F. Buckley and how Vidal suspected and feared that Buckley had evidence with which to blackmail him. Till now I'd more or less taken Vidal at his word, in his memoir *Palimpsest* and elsewhere, when he described his lifelong pining for the one boy he truly loved: Jimmie Trimble, a classmate who was later killed in World War II. And I believed his repeated proclamations that the key to his fifty-three-year partnership with Howard Austen was "no sex." Well, Tim really "unpacks," as academics like to say, these latter two well-polished myths, and I can no longer accept them—or Vidal—as I once did. In short, *In Bed with Gore Vidal* is the most complete and unguarded look at Vidal's life that we've ever had. Most of us will see him in a new light, one that won't necessarily flatter him or support his side of the story.

Despite my misgivings, I didn't think it was possible for me to feel anything but uncritical adoration for Vidal because he gave me my real start as an editor. For this, I'll be eternally indebted to him. In an incredibly generous move he had nothing to gain from, he agreed to let me—a total stranger with no formal editorial training who worked at a small San Francisco press—collect his essays on sex into a book I called *Sexually Speaking*. Unlike Vidal's fiction, which sometimes was too clever and out of touch, I felt, with readers, his essays uniformly delighted me. Regardless of topic, I could read his essays over and over. In fact I did, which is how *Sexually Speaking* came about. After countless re-readings, I had a special fondness for his pieces on sex and sexual politics (those on Nasser's Egypt and Barry Goldwater, less so). I couldn't think of anyone who matched Vidal's wit and intelligence on the topic of sex—I still don't think anyone does—so I came up with the idea of publishing a book devoted to just these writings. I suppose, being young at the time, everything, including working with Vidal, felt within reach. I got his address in Ravello, Italy, from a non-profit group he'd done a fundraiser for, and mailed the table of contents along with a letter of introduction to his home. About a week later a fax was waiting for me at the office, written in his own hand: "Dear Donald Weise, Yes I will do your book. Contact my agent at the number below." It was the biggest moment in my life up to that point, and may still be. Gore Vidal—the impossibly forbidding and imposing literary giant—said yes to me.

As if working with one of my celebrity icons so suddenly and unexpectedly weren't enough, I wrote and asked if I could come to Ravello and interview him about sex: an interview which would appear at the end of the book as sort of a culmination of his lifetime writing on the topic. In some cases twenty-five years had passed since he'd written these essays, and I wanted him to weigh in on where he stood now. He said yes again. And a few months later I was in Italy, sitting with Vidal in his home talking about sex.

I prepared for this meeting with the determination of an Olympic athlete. I re-read many of Vidal's novels, went through his plays, read all the essays again at least twice, tracked down documentary films about him on video, and I even watched the old movies he'd written or at least had a hand in writing, like *Ben Hur* and *Catered Affair*. I wanted to be able to reference anything that might come up about any of his work because this interview quite literally meant the world to me. I'd been trying to get my foot in the door as an editor for a while but hadn't had any help. Now here was the opportunity of a lifetime. I prepared so intensively for the visit because it was about more than just publishing his book of essays or trying to make a good in-person impression on Vidal. That trip was the start of my career, and I was lucky enough for it to open like a fairy tale, thanks to him.

Although I'd seen him in person at book signings and public talks, there in Ravello, I was thoroughly intimidated from the moment I shook his hand. He was wearing a brown jogging suit and looked like he hadn't shaved for days, reminding me of how my grandfather looked in the hospital. I followed him inside his villa, through the foyer, down a long tiled hallway, and into a handsome living room that I had seen photographed in magazines. He went to one of the windows and pulled open a large curtain that revealed a breath-taking view of the Gulf of Salerno far below. Vidal then pointed out the island where Nureyev once lived and reminisced about Nureyev coming to swim in his pool. I gathered this overture was one he performed for all wide-eyed newcomers like me, and if it was meant to put me at ease, that was immediately undone when I turned and saw behind us a row of elegantly framed photographs along a table—signed portraits of Eleanor Roosevelt, Jacqueline Kennedy, and Amelia Earhart prominent among them.

With the view properly taken in, we went to a less formal but similarly elegant room where Vidal did all his writing when in Italy, he said. We settled into big leather chairs opposite one another, a floor-to-ceiling wall of books behind me. I set out my tape recorder on the table between us to begin the interview. Having never interviewed anyone before, I'd typed up a list of about twenty-five, overly detailed questions that must have run more than twenty pages. What I was thinking when I came up with them all or what I was expecting Vidal to endure that day, I can't say. I was incredibly earnest, however, and wanted to demonstrate I could be taken seriously as an editor. The fact that I had mistakenly put on one black sock and one white sock before I left the hotel that day would, I feared, signal otherwise. My questions ranged broadly—over history, politics, and literature, mostly—and his often hilarious off-the-cuff answers sounded exactly as you'd expect:

On ancient Greece: "The Greeks never had a word for 'faggot' or 'dyke'; the concepts didn't exist. They knew about feminine men and sometimes thought they were funny—more 'ha-ha' than peculiar. They certainly knew about lust; they didn't make a fuss about it. This was a world I understood and was brought up in: it was, sexually, extremely free. Homosexuality was institutionalized, because it was useful for training soldiers—in Thebes and Sparta specifically. You also got married to have children so there would be more babies. It never occurred to people you would be one thing or the other."

On sexual guilt: "As I said to Ian McKellen, 'I've never had a moment of sexual guilt,' and he said, 'I bet you haven't.' If you're brought up in the house of a senator you're not going to be very concerned about what a postal worker thinks of your private life."

On Eleanor Roosevelt: "It was perfectly clear [reading the private correspondence between Roosevelt and her long-rumored lover Lorena Hickok] that they were having sex. The writing is full of tactile images which are erotic. . . . On the topic of sex, she didn't like anything about it. And when she said 'sex' she meant hetero sex. She had these funny veins in her temple that would pop out like serpents when the subject of sex came up. She was very non-judgmental about others: 'People are what they are; there's nothing you can do.'"

On James Baldwin: "Along comes Jimmy Baldwin of all people who accuses me of homosexual panic. If ever there was a book of homosexual panic it was *Giovanni's Room*. What is this homosexual panic? Bob Ford [in *The City and the Pillar*] suffers from it, and rejects the other one because of it, and gets himself beaten up because of it. But there was no 'panic' on the part of the writer, which should have been perfectly clear to Jimmy, although he wasn't clear headed. . . . He had more to carry than any writer I know. A black writer who then turns out to be a queen and also a preacher of the Lord; it was one of the reasons he was so often hysterical and very often made no sense at all, because he was living too many contradictions."

On Dr. Alfred Kinsey: "Kinsey found that thirty-seven percent of men had had a sexual experience with another male to the point of ejaculation. Well, the intellectuals moaned and whined at these findings. They asked, 'How do you measure sex by ejaculation?' 'How else do you measure it? There is no way of measuring love, compassion, and goodness and all that you value and I value. I'm a scientist and I have to have something to measure and *that's* something'. . . . They did a recent survey, and they now have it down to one percent, one percent of males have had a same-sex experience. That's so palpably a lie. It had middle-class women asking people questions. No one is going to tell these ladies that 'I'm not going to touch you with a ten-foot barge-pole; you are absolutely safe from me and my kind.' It's just an embarrassing situation, and they confessed to having a lot of non-responses."

On gay novelists: "There are certainly people who call themselves 'gay novelists' like Edmund White. I think he's out of his mind. Why limit yourself any more than literature has limited you? In a world where people don't read, what are you going to make of a man who calls himself a 'gay novelist'? What's that supposed to mean, that he's only going to write about cock? He's a quite good writer, but I didn't think he was that dumb to characterize himself."

We spoke for about three hours, and while there wasn't enough time to go through my complete list of questions (even after three hours!), he'd given me enough material for an extraordinary interview.

As the afternoon wore on, Vidal's answers became shorter and shorter. I took this to be a sign of him tiring—of answering questions and maybe even of having me there. I didn't drink at the time so I couldn't appreciate the fact that evening approaching meant the first drink of the day. Almost at five o'clock on the nose he said, "I'd like a drink." He went over to the bar and returned with two glasses of Scotch, something I'd never had before. He then turned on the television and said, not waiting for a reply, "If you don't mind, I'm following the hearings and they're about to start." The hearings were the Senate hearings to impeach President Clinton.

At this moment—as if on cue—his red-haired partner of forty-odd years, Howard Austen, walked into the room wearing a terrycloth bathrobe and made his way straight for the bar. I don't remember if I was introduced to Howard, whom I'd recognized from pictures, but Vidal, holding up the book of nude photographs I'd brought as a gift, said to him, "Look, Don brought us a dirty book." While Howard paged through the book over his cocktail, the live hearings started on TV. Talking with Vidal in his home all afternoon about sex was surreal enough, but watching an event as historic as a Senate hearing to impeach the president was even more so. I stayed quiet and just listened as he kept up a near-constant conversation with the proceedings on TV, critiquing one Republican senator after the next, saying over and over how senators hated to be lectured by one another. He was as bawdy and as outspoken and outraged as you'd imagine. After a young male Republican senator finished condemning the President at length, Vidal said, "Well, that's the mouth of a cocksucker if ever I saw one."

After a while I noticed it had gotten dark outside. The liquor kept coming and there was no sign of food, but I didn't know at what point I was expected to leave. Finally Vidal made a phone call and said his driver would take me back down the hill to my hotel in Amalfi whenever I was ready, which I took to mean *now*. I thanked him profusely for his time and cooperation as he walked me back to the gate. I'm glad he led the way. Given how much I'd had to drink, I might have wandered around the grounds all night trying to find the exit in the dark.

As it happened, Vidal later decided not to include our interview in the book. I don't know if he felt he'd given away too much material for free or that he said a handful of personal comments that he now believed were too revealing—about his father, for example—but he changed his mind. Not at first, though. After I'd gotten home, a call came one afternoon when I was alone in the office. The voice on the other end said simply, "Gore Vidal," as if answering a question. I'd gotten a lot of queries from strangers about how to get in touch with him once it became known that I was publishing his book, and I took this to be yet another. I said Gore Vidal wasn't there, that the caller had reached his publisher. "No," said what can only be described as a commanding voice, "This *is* Gore Vidal." Panicked, I grabbed the nearest pen and paper, prepared to take down anything he said. He was phoning about the interview; he had changes. "Where I call Jimmy Baldwin a drunk, strike that," he told me, then proceeded to go through the transcription I'd sent him, making further cuts that dramatically shortened the piece, much to my distress. I'd never been so nervous or caught off guard, and the whole time a voice inside me kept saying, "You're in over your head! Who do you think you are, working with Gore Vidal?" Where I came from nobody met anyone who'd written a book or spoke with anybody who'd ever appeared on TV. But I stayed right with him, writing as fast as I could, not daring to ask him to repeat himself or slow down. Regardless of his cuts, however, he chose in the end to drop our piece entirely. So I'd held onto the interview tapes for years, thinking one day, after his death, I'd publish them somewhere.

Which brings me back to *In Bed with Gore Vidal*. As Tim made progress on the book, he shared with me one piece of exciting news after the next. Someone he'd been doggedly trailing for weeks gave in for an interview. That person in turn put Tim in touch with still another source close to Vidal. Unpublished material from Vidal's first biography, which was never completed or released due to the author's death, was made available to Tim. From the outside it all looked so easy, but for Tim, I can only imagine how much time and energy had to be invested to achieve these incredible results. Finally I had his amazing manuscript in my hands. It was so good, in fact, that I decided to give him my interview tapes for the book, because whatever plans I had for them couldn't compare to their importance in helping to tell Vidal's story in this groundbreaking biography. I felt I owed it to Tim—although, oddly, to Vidal, as well.

Before giving Tim the tapes, however, I listened to them for the first time in fifteen years, curious to know if I'd remembered our talk accurately. For the most part, yes. I remember commenting on the framed *Time* magazine cover from the 1960's on the wall behind him honoring his then-new novel *Myra Breckinridge*, which led him to talk about the flood of fan mail from transsexuals following the book's publication, graphic photos included, he said. I remembered him impersonating President Kennedy and Eleanor Roosevelt, priceless recordings that are sadly lost on the printed page. What I didn't remember was interrupting him as often as I do in the tapes, or how forthright I was at times.

After listening to our conversation I found myself regretting more than ever Vidal's decision not to include even an abbreviated version of our interview in *Sexually Speaking*, which became a *Los Angeles Times* best seller. (When one of my mother's friends saw the *Times* list and told her the news, my mother phoned me and said, "The book you did with your friend is on the best seller list." Even today, Vidal, for all his fame and accomplishments, is known to her alone as "my friend.") Vidal himself never told me what he thought of the book, though he did agree to one public event to promote it.

He was visiting San Francisco to plug his latest novel and said he'd do an event in the Castro as I'd asked if I set one up. The local Metropolitan Community Church was more than delighted to host. I was to introduce Vidal and then he would speak onstage by himself. But a half hour before the event I got a phone call from his publicist telling me Vidal expected me to interview him in front of the audience. I was nervous as usual in Vidal's presence—made all the more so because the church was packed, as if it were a revival. From nerves, I ad libbed my opening remark: "I never thought I'd be sitting in church with Gore Vidal." This in turn led to my first question: "So when was the last time you were in church?" Without missing a beat, Vidal said, "The pope's funeral. I wanted to make sure he was dead." It went on like that for the next hour, and how I wish that conversation had been taped, too.

So to answer my own question, what do I think of a biography of Vidal that looks at his life with complete honesty, showing all his shortcomings and personal contradictions for the first time? I feel this is a tremendous gift toward understanding the man and his work. While recalling the legend may be fun—quoting his outrageous remarks or watching vintage clips of Vidal on YouTube—it ultimately obscures the man behind the writing. Some of Vidal's concerns—like his lifelong preoccupation with his fame—aren't flattering for me, and I feel both disappointed that Vidal was so self-absorbed and sympathetic toward his burning need for adulation. In a sense, *In Bed with Gore Vidal* puts the pieces of his life's puzzle together without lessening the essential mysteries of his great talent and his flinty, unusual character.

LAWRENCE SCHIMEL

A MIDSUMMER NIGHT'S PRESS

LAWRENCE SCHIMEL writes in both Spanish and English and has published over 100 books in many different genres, including the poetry collections *Desayuno en la cama* (Egales, 2008), *Fairy Tales for Writers* (A Midsummer Night's Press, 2007) and *Deleted Names* (A Midsummer Night's Press, 2013), among many others. His poetry has been published in a broad array of periodicals, both queer (*Bay Windows, Windy City Times, Gay Scotland*, etc.) and mainstream (*The Saturday Evening Post, The Christian Science Monitor, Physics Today*, etc.) and have been widely anthologized, again in both in queer (*Gay Love Poetry, Queer Dog: Homo/Pup/Poems, Blanco Nuclear*, etc.) and mainstream (*The Random House Treasury of Light Verse, Chicken Soup for the Horse-Lover's Soul 2*, etc.) collections. He has won the Lambda Literary Award (twice), the Independent Publisher Book Award, and the Spectrum Award, among other honors. Since 1999, he has lived in Madrid, Spain, where he works as a Spanish-to-English translator.

As an editor, he has published numerous anthologies, in many different genres, many of them focused on LGBT writing. His very first book, published in 1995, was the anthology of gay poetry *The Badboy Book of Erotic Poetry* (Badboy), published under the pseudonym David Laurents, which was a finalist for the Lambda Literary Award. Other anthologies of gay poetry that he has edited, under his own name, include *Best*

Gay Poetry 2008 (A Midsummer Night's Press) and, in Catalan, *Ells s'estimen: Poemes d'amor entre homes* (Llibres de L'Index, 1999).

A Midsummer Night's Press was started in 1991 when he began publishing poetry broadsides on a letterpress in the basement of his dorm at Yale University. It went on hiatus when he graduated and lost access to the press, starting up again in 1997 when the press began to publish professionally printed books, primarily under two imprints: Fabula Rasa, devoted to mythic poetry and fairy tale retellings, and Body Language, devoted to poetry by LGBT voices. Nearly half of the 16 books it has published to date have been first collections. Queer poets the press has published include: David Bergman, Julie R. Enszer, Raymond Luczak, Roz Kaveney, Michael Broder, Brane Mozetic, and Julie Marie Wade. A Midsummer Night's Press also co-publishes the Sapphic Classics series with *Sinister Wisdom* magazine, reissuing important lesbian poetry collections with new introductions and other materials to contextualize these iconic texts for a new audience. The first two titles in this series are *Crime Against Nature* by Minnie Bruce Pratt and *Living as a Lesbian* by Cheryl Clarke.

Q: What advice would you give to an editor early in his or her career?

I am a very hands-on editor, I think, and am not afraid to take a manuscript apart and put it back together again, often asking a poet to cut pieces or add more, or to revise poems on a line-by-line basis. That said, I think one of the most important things for an editor to learn is how to encourage a writer to help push them to create the best work they're capable of. Sometimes this involves teasing it out of the author and sometimes it involves nagging and bullying, and the trick is to learn how to handle each individual author-editor relationship.

At the same time, I think that asking questions of the author is a helpful device. And also: letting the author know when something doesn't work, or you don't understand something, and then letting the author go in and try to fix it. The editor's job is often more to find where the manuscript or an individual poem/ piece of prose doesn't work, and then it's up to the author to figure out how to resolve it. An editor can have suggestions but needs to let the author resolve it in a way that may be different from what the editor had in mind.

LONELY PLANET

You fuck like a tourist:
you're in a rush to visit
the main attractions
following the itinerary recommended
in the guidebooks, not because you're interested
in each stop but in order to later
be able to tell your friends
that you've done them.

I should've realized
when you approached me in the bar
that, although you're from here, you've got
thousands of frequent flyer miles
under your belt.

You've seen so many paintings, so many bodies,
that you no longer look, my nakedness unfolded
like a map before you. But this map
is missing the "You Are Here" arrow because
you are somewhere else, maybe thinking of
what souvenirs you'll buy in the gift shop,
what stories you'll tell about our encounter,

and I feel like a foreigner in my own bed.

AUTOPSY

I don't plan to die of love.
But I'm sure that
if they open my body right now
they'd discover some organ
I didn't have before
and which hurts me so much now.

Maybe it's not new for science
but it is for me:
something my body has produced
only since I met you,
since I continue waiting for any response
from you.

POSSESSIVE

I feel jealous, on visiting a friend
and seeing on his nightstand
a book I loaned him

like running into, on the street, a guy
you've tricked with
holding hands with someone else.

RECIPE FOR LOVE

I can never cook from a book:
all exact and impersonal measurements.
I need someone to show me,
step by step, how it's done.

I'm a lazy cook; I didn't begin
to experiment, to explore, until I was no longer cooking
only for myself.

Let's add a pinch
of this, we'll cook by taste, trying every while
what we're preparing. We'll feed
one another. If something's missing
we'll improvise.

Everything I know about cooking I learned from a friend
who told me: the secret to cooking is to never let
the food smell your fear.

It's also all I know about love.

Let's go into the kitchen
and I'll show you.

AIDS LIMERICKS

Denying the End

These hospital visits portend
That death very soon will attend
    This friend with bold face
    And bear-hug embrace
Who begs that I please just pretend.

Lights Out

My life has become a motif
of daily compassion and grief,
    of watching the ends
    of lovers and friends
whose candles have been far too brief.

SKATING BEAUTY

Like the uninvited
thirteenth fairy at the christening,
I am standing just outside
the plaza where they're skating

and I want to curse them
for my not being a part
of such easy youthful
masculine fellowship.

Forget the prick of a finger
on a spinning wheel's needle,
let them crush their hands
beneath the spinning wheels

of their skateboards!
But I want more than just
belonging; it is you I crave:
a beauty that could exist

only in fairy tale,
where magic or alchemy
transforms a catalogue of parts—
eyes, lips, lithe torso that twists

just so at the waist—into something
wondrous and unique, delicate and fierce,
hovering on that threshold
between boyhood and manhood.

Almost shy when on the ground,
unaware of your own desirability,
your board, tucked under your arm
like a shield, blocks the view of your

naked torso as you constantly shift
position, less nervousness than
restless excess of energy.
Then you mount your board.

Everything changes: you are
a modern-day centaur, board and boy
a single being whose grace
and almost preternatural calm

draws the attention of every eye.
Suddenly you launch into the air
legs bent at the knees. You soar,
your board flying up beneath you

and time stops

                for a hundred years

with you suspended in this moment

and only a kiss from me
could make it start again.

[ON THE STREET, AT THE CORNER]

On the street, at the corner,
we kiss one another.

It's different from the heated kisses
we gave one another inside,
as we fucked in a cubicle.

We've already exchanged phone numbers
after having exchanged fluids.

To kiss a guy on the street is different
from kissing him goodnight in bed
knowing he'll still be there when you wake up.

This is a kiss full of promises,
a kiss of possibilities, a kiss
full of future.

I resist the impulse to look back
and smile to myself during the walk
back home, with your taste on my lips.

[I TRY TO WRITE SOMETHING NICE ABOUT OUR RELATIONSHIP]

I try to write something nice about our relationship,
but the page remains blank.

We've had sex, we've offered and received pleasure
from our bodies. But I don't know how to transform
those moments
into poems.

I lift my gaze. A guy, also alone, seated
at another table, is looking at me. He smiles when he sees
that I've seen him looking at me.
Maybe now is not the moment
for either poems or the past.

[THE NIGHT HAS CHANGED BUT]

The night has changed but
it has not changed. The same faces,
sometimes: those guys who live
in Never Land. And other
faces that look the same.
There are new boys, but they are
the same age we were then.

Where have all the guys gone
who, like me, have grown up,
who have entered another world
and are now exiled from the night
like shadows come un-attached
from their bodies? Every time
I go out at night

I ask myself: are we beings
searching for our shadows
or shadows fleeing
from ourselves?

[WE HAD ALL THE INGREDIENTS]

We had all the ingredients
for a romantic moment:

the full moon reflected in the sea,
his arms wrapped around me from behind

as we smoked on the balcony.
Only missing was love, that spark.

It's not that I wanted someone else
but neither did I want him.

What am I doing here? Why
am I forcing this to work?

I think that I am trying to prove
something—but I don't know what exactly, nor

to whom, although I suspect that it is
to myself. A shiver runs through

me. "The sea breeze," I tell him,
when he notices the spasm.

We go inside. We go to his bedroom
and fuck, holding back our shouts

so as not to wake his roommate.

SINISTER LOVE

I don't know what's happened, how we've come to this.
How is it that we can no longer find the love
we felt for one another?
I know that I still love you. Everything else is just details.

Something needs to change.

I write this poem with my left hand.
Although I can barely decipher my own handwriting,
perhaps this way I can break this cycle of mutual
recriminations and see things another way,
can rediscover the love we feel.

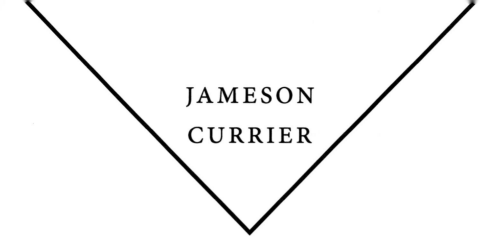

CHELSEA STATION EDITIONS

JAMESON CURRIER's stories, poems, reviews, essays, interviews, and articles on AIDS and gay culture have been published in many national and local publications, anthologies, websites, magazines, and literary journals. He is the author of five novels and four collections of short fiction that deal in whole or in part with the impact of the AIDS epidemic on gay lives. In 2010 he founded Chelsea Station Editions, an independent press devoted to gay literature. Books published by the press have been honored by the Lambda Literary Foundation, the American Library Association GLBT Round Table, the Saints and Sinners Literary Festival, the Gaylactic Spectrum Awards Foundation, and the Rainbow Book Awards. In 2011, he launched the literary magazine *Chelsea Station*, which has published the works of more than a hundred writers. In 2013, he edited two new anthologies featuring original work: *With: New Gay Fiction* and *Between: New Gay Poetry*. Born in the South, he continues to reside in New York.

Q: What is the publisher's greatest responsibility?

One of the reasons why I am a publisher has a lot to do with being an author. Early in my writing career I joined a gay men's writing group in Manhattan. Among the other members was David Feinberg, who at the time was writing the humorous pieces that would become part of his novel Eighty-Sixed. *I was writing short stories about the impact of AIDS on the lives of gay men at a time when few other gay writers were doing so, and David was very appreciative and admiring of what I was trying to accomplish. Unbeknownst to me, David gave some of my short stories to his editor at Viking Penguin who had optioned* Eighty-Sixed *and that was how my first collection of short stories,* Dancing on the Moon, *came to be published. It was the most generous thing one writer could do for another, and to this day I still fall to tears when I think of what it meant to my own writing career. And that is what I try to pass along today as a writer, editor, and publisher. A generosity to other writers. Of understanding what it is to research and strive and practice and create, of understanding another writer's purpose and mission and goals, of loving and admiring someone else's writing so much that I will do all I can to see that it is read by others.*

CHELSEA

The bus stops every two blocks
from here to there.
I no longer get off, though,
at the street where he once lived.
I see him in every passenger now:
one man has his eyebrows,
another the shape of his jaw,
a woman has his smile,
a boy wears his glasses—
at the curb I see a man with his walk.
I see him in stores
and in the line at the bank,
a girl wears his coat,
another his cap.

I see him at the movies
and at the office,
flashing by me in taxis and on bikes.
Not even forty, I have reached the age
where the dead outnumber the living,
old faces imprinted on indifferent strangers,
every glance leaves me wanting to say,
hello, how are you?
I've missed you,
I haven't seen you in a while.
The bus still stops every two blocks
as if nothing has changed;
people get on and off,
some going home, others away.
I have reached a place I never set out for;
death, my companion, without any warning.
When Kevin left I lost my joy,
with Peter went my patience;
by the time Mark died I had even lost my anger.
Living, now, seems a series of false hopes:
AZT, macrobiotics, crystals, and prayer.
Every day something else is lost,
every new death leaves me thinking of the past.
But I still ride the bus from here to there,
traveling no longer to learn or to experience,
hoping, instead, I won't forget my life.
All these stops have made me wiser,
but leave me less happy.
This, then, is the order in which they got off:
Kevin, Sam, George, Mark, and David.

AT THE GATES OF THE CIRCUS

Just after the first snow had melted
and froze into a glaze of ice,
we went to the circus
uptown near Lincoln Center.

He had trouble walking that night,
not just from the ice—
he had lost too much weight,
the lesions taken hold of him.

He refused the cane I bought him,
refused my arm for support, too.
Dignity showing its colors, I knew.
Vanity proving its pride.

As we approached the entrance,
strings of lights illuminated the gates.
A cold wind blew between us,
our heads bowed as if in prayer.

It was then I lost my balance
on a patch of ice,
and reaching out for support
I found his arm.

He caught me before I fell,
Saving *me* from embarrassment.
Isn't it romantic, he said,
lifting me with his smile.

ROCK HUDSON'S VACATION

When Rock Hudson died at his home in Los Angeles in October 1985 at the age of fifty-nine, his death created a transformation in the public consciousness of AIDS. Though he was the first major public figure to openly acknowledge that he was suffering from the illness, his last days were not without sensation and scandal. Speculation about his health began earlier that year when he appeared thin and frail during a taping of a cable television program hosted by his former co-star Doris Day. News reports during the summer had him collapsing at a hotel in Paris where he had gone to seek medical treatment, and, soon thereafter, stories began to appear of the actor's secret gay life in Hollywood. Not long after that, and only a few weeks before his death, Hudson released a statement at an AIDS fundraiser in Los Angeles that read: "I am not happy that I am sick. I am not happy that I have AIDS, but if that is helping others, I can, at least, know that my own misfortune has had some positive worth."

Rock Hudson's closeted gay life was not so secret to many people; like the sexual activity of many other gay entertainers (Liberace, Tony Perkins, and Montgomery Clift), Hudson's homosexuality was generally known and accepted in the entertainment industry and gay community and, in the days before media "outing," protected by the goodwill of both. Five years before his death from AIDS, I met Rock Hudson at the opening night party of a Broadway musical that I was working on as an apprentice publicist. The black-tie affair was at an Upper West Side restaurant near Lincoln Center. Hudson and his partner at the time were friendly with two women I worked for, and I was introduced to the actor while he was seated at a table with his friends. One of my bosses was also seated at the table, and as I leaned down to whisper a question in her ear, she turned to the man next to her and said, "Rock, this is my assistant." I tilted my head and my eyes met his briefly. He smiled and I blushed, but before anything else could be said, my boss was standing up from her chair, pushing me out into the room, and giving me instructions to assemble the cast for a photograph. I was twenty-five years old that year and still a wide-eyed newcomer to New York City and the Broadway theater, and I did not let the opportunity pass to find some kind of a detail of the man who was an American icon which I could pass along to my friends and family. In my recollection of that night, I realize exactly how young and boyish I was, amazed simply by the actor's towering height when he stood up from the table to leave the party. He was heavy-shouldered and six foot four, and it was clear to me why he had made it in Hollywood—he still carried the handsome ruggedness that had made him a legend.

I am not even a minor character in Rock Hudson's story. My meeting is not revealed as any anecdote in any biographies of the actor or the reminiscences of his friends. He was never an idol to me. I didn't think much of the films he made with Doris Day—there was always something so implausible to them—though I came to admire his films more in the years after his death, my favorite being *Giant* because of its epic quality. Rock Hudson was more a part of my parents' generation than my own. And, as I recall, the year that I met him I was more enamored with the likes of Richard Gere and Jack Wrangler.

I must backtrack, however, to explain how I found my first job in the New York theater. After college, I moved from Atlanta to Manhattan with the dual purpose of attending graduate school and exploring my attraction toward men away from the scrutiny of my family and a hometown girlfriend. At New York University, where I was studying in the Drama department, I met my first gay friend in the city, an editor for a show business trade paper who was involved with a man who worked as a theatrical publicist and whose office was looking for a gofer. At the time, I was working a few hours a week as a telephone answering service operator used primarily by actors, and the money I had taken out in loans for graduate school and my move north was quickly drying up. I thought a full-time job would help get my finances in better shape, and, if the truth be known, the lure of working in the professional theater was too heady to resist. I loved the theater and desperately wanted to be a part of it. As a young man in Atlanta I had performed in summer stock productions, built sets for productions that played the Civic Center, directed large-scale university productions, and toured shopping malls, high schools, and retirement homes singing with a cabaret troupe. My interview with the woman who co-owned the entertainment publicity firm was brusque and brief. I was hired on the spot, not because I was young and eager and smart and came with theatrical experience and a recommendation, but because I could spell and type without too many mistakes. (This was the era of carbon paper and bottles of white-out, three copies of everything typed at once.)

My daily duties at the new job included canvassing the newspapers and magazines that arrived in the office to find tearsheets and clippings that mentioned clients and shows the agency represented. I was so naive to the business of show business that I was not even aware that the city sported three daily newspapers or that there were such things as theater critics for television networks. I was taught how to fold a printed press release and the correct way to insert it into an envelope (headline side up), as well as how to seal only half of the flap on the back so that it would be easier to open by the recipient. The two co-owners of the agency, their one associate, and I sat in the same room with our desks facing each other so that our interactions were both effortless and annoying. I was to answer the phone before it reached its second ring, even if I was talking on another line. In the mornings, I made coffee before anyone else arrived, and at lunch time, if there were no pressing engagements for the owners with a producer or a reporter, I brought back pastrami or tongue sandwiches from the deli across the street. At night, I delivered ticket requests to the box office and messages to backstage doormen of the theaters where the office had shows running or clients performing. I typed names on envelopes, licked rolls of stamps, and carted bags of mail to the post office. It was one of those jobs that makes you question why you went to college in the first place, and so it was no surprise that I surprised myself and dropped out of graduate school because I felt that, well, as silly as it sounds, I was learning a lot more from working in the theater than I was by studying it in a textbook.

The main partner of the agency, the taller and older of the two women, was a mannish lady with a penchant for long mink coats and cowboy accessories—pointed toe boots, large engraved belt buckles, and Stetson hats. She had worked in the publicity business for more than thirty years and was full of a wisdom she felt necessary to direct toward others, particularly me, since I was in such close earshot of her booming voice. She had originally hoped to be an actress, but during rehearsals for a show she tripped on an imaginary flight of stairs and broke her collarbone and, as luck had it, ended up working in a publicity office where she began by typing, answering phones, and reading the papers, just as I was doing. Years of smoking had left her with a hacking cough and a deep, phlegmy rasp, which she would transform into a girlish tone when on the phone, trying to place a story with an editor or columnist. Her partner was a short, younger Italian woman with manicured nails and a teased hairstyle that made her pale face seem surrounded by a pair of large, dark raven's wings. She was the novice publicist of the two owners but the sharper businesswoman when it came to keeping the office running and the books balanced, and she spent hours refusing to take phone calls while she punched the keys of a calculator with the eraser tip of a pencil, the chug-chug-chug of its motor spitting out a long ribbon of paper.

I did not know that these two women were lovers when I first began working in the office, but it was not difficult to realize it after a day or so of their temperamental activity toward each other. They were big New York City creations—butch and femme—two self-made successes with a few family pedigrees thrown in, who shared an apartment on Park Avenue, a summer home in Connecticut, and a Mercedes Benz which they housed in either east or west side garages, depending on what side of town they were on at the time. In addition to their celebrity clients and Broadway productions, they had a Rolodex of high-profile friends, gay and otherwise, culled not only from the theater community but also from the fashion industry and the media. On New Year's Eve, they threw an annual party where black tie was *de rigeur* and the likes of Rex Reed, Ann Miller, Lana Cantrell, Liz Smith, and Ethel Merman might be spotted and which, once I had paid my dues in overtime hours, I was also expected to attend, even though I was decades younger than most of the other guests.

I soon found that there were other young gay men working in the support industries of the Broadway community training to become company managers or house managers or press agents. Many of them became close friends when we began to gossip of the bizarre behavior of our employers or clients. We would swap tickets to each other's shows the same way straight boys would swap baseball cards and invite each other to opening night parties where we were not expected to work because we were not there for a client but could, instead, find ourselves locked in the embrace of a waiter in the stall of a downstairs bathroom for a few brief minutes of unexpected pleasure. It was a heady time to be young and gay and working behind the scenes. My story, however, and my years of working in the theater, is not that of someone who might have bartended at Studio 54 and found sex and drugs and a kind of celebrity for himself. It is the story of young man trying to understand a quirky business and who is always overworked but aware that there is something special around the next corner that he has never before seen or done or known about, so he puts up with a little more than he might have if he was older and wiser. One night, for instance, I *could* make it inside the velvet ropes of Studio 54 and watch Andy Warhol's coterie arrive because a friend of a friend had passed along a VIP ticket for that night, or another night, I might have to work and show up late at the theater to escort a press photographer into a backstage dressing room when Robert Redford congratulated the cast. The list of people I worked with and met is extraordinary for its time: Truman Capote, Kathy Bates, John Travolta, Eve Arden, Geraldine Page, Celeste Holm. Harvey Fierstein sent me a Christmas card. Elizabeth Ashley pressed a bandage against my forehead one evening after I had been injured while preventing a mugging. I once had a conversation with fashion designer Donald Brooks about the shoes I was wearing, a pair of gray suede platforms I had brought with me from Atlanta.

I've often avoided talking about my work in the theater because I felt that it could easily overshadow other aspects of my life. I am also somewhat embarrassed by this past obsessiveness of mine to belong and be a part of the theater, as well as the large amount of faith that I invested in it, hoping it would lead me to find myself, and which is why, when the novelty of this job wore off, I found that I was fighting a cynicism that was bitter even by New York standards. And it's hard for me to admit, too, that I invested a great deal of time and energy trying to prove myself in a career in public relations that I soon discovered I was ill-suited for, whether it was in the theater or in a corporate environment. But that is not to say that those years were without fond memories or deeper discoveries about the direction I wanted to take my life. This, too, requires a bit of backtracking to explain.

By the end of my eighth month working in the publicity office, I began a three-year apprenticeship to join the union which represented the theatrical press agents and managers. It would be a long struggle for me to complete this because I had added up the pluses and minuses and found my heart was only half in the job. The apprenticeship was low paying, my bosses were jealous and vengeful, and, while I continued being the office gofer, I was now juggling added responsibilities—writing press releases, setting up interviews, helping with the details of opening night performances and parties. Occasionally, there would be some other person brought in to help out in the office, but generally the budget was small and limited and the new help that was found was not necessarily interested in starting at a rung that was well beneath the basement floor. The associate who had found me the job was gone before I began my apprenticeship, and another associate packed up his bags when a show he was working on folded; another came in and found no problem with having the young kid do his work for him until it was time for him to leave as well, which left the agency essentially a three-person operation—the two older women (the bosses) and myself (the hired help who kept things going).

You may notice that I have not identified my employers by name. It would be years before I could acknowledge the damage to my self-esteem they had caused. Sometimes I think that I watched my youth disappear during this time—I always seemed to be working, dragging myself into the office on weekends to update a list of press contacts, repair a release I had fudged, or cover an event that was happening at a theater. I was also rock bottom poor. The money I earned from my apprenticeship was not enough to pay my rent. I often walked thirty blocks to work to save money. Many days I skipped lunch. I was lucky that I answered the phone at work so I could hang up on the credit card companies tracking me down about missing a monthly payment without my bosses knowing how bad my finances were. As I look back on those years, however, I do see that I had dates and affairs (though no one serious emerged), and I explored gay life with my friends with the same curiosity I was investing in the theater. I went to the bars, beaches, and the baths, hitched trips with friends to Fire Island and the Hamptons, took buses to Provincetown and Atlantic City, but it always seemed that I had this job to come back to that I didn't like but everyone else thought was wonderful. At times I wished I were older because then I thought I might be able to take my life more seriously and that others might regard me as someone other than the kid who worked in the office. For a while I grew a beard in hopes that it would make me look older, but the truth of it was, I looked, instead, like a boyish man impersonating an older one.

It was during this time that the two women I worked for began talking about a vacation that they would be taking around the upcoming end-of-the-year holidays. As a rule, they did not take vacations and loved to remind me of the fact when I dreamed of taking one myself. (There are no holidays in the theater, my bosses liked to tell me, only added performances.) The women did, however, maintain a three-day work week during the summer months, which essentially gave them four consecutive days at their country house. My work schedule during those summer months remained the same, however—always available and always on call and always trying to cover the fact that they were not in the office and not available to take anyone's call. Their upcoming holiday vacation was a Caribbean cruise on a private yacht with several friends, among them, as I recall, Claire Trevor, Ross Hunter, and Rock Hudson and his partner. At the time I thought it was a luxury to have them out of the office. They were eager to get away from the relentless pull of the theater and work, and I was eager to see them go. My bosses were big drinkers and I imagined their celebrity friends to be as well, and when the day of their departure arrived, I visualized them lounging in recliners and sipping exotic drinks, attended by smartly dressed sailors and cabin boys. *Bon voyage*, I said to them on the phone. (And please don't bother me while you are away.)

By then, the day they left for their cruise, I had fully recognized the mistake I had made in continuing with this publicity job, but I was also becoming aware of who I wanted to become. I had decided I wanted to be a writer. I did not see my own life as something to write about, so for inspiration I had become enamored with the idea of writing down the anecdotes of a friend who was an itinerant actress and musician and her travels with a small group of musical performers around the country. I was writing my first novel. I had started reading more to learn the structure behind fiction, started constructing my friend's anecdotes into tales and then stories and chapters of a novel. And I could not get this idea or this desire or these characters out of my head until I had put them on paper. They pursued me down the street, waited with me while I delivered messages or asked questions about interviews, and held press tickets in my hand. I recall one day being tugged away from my responsibilities in the office and toward the typewriter by one of my characters chattering away in my mind, and I started typing away at my desk, only to be asked in a suspicious tone by one of my bosses what the hell it was that I was so furiously at work on. I made up a lie, telling her that I was writing down some column ideas I had heard. (After that, in the office, I only wrote notes on scraps of paper while answering the phones, everything typed up later at home.)

So when my bosses left for their vacation with Rock Hudson, my immediate reaction was *Hooray!* I would have more freedom to write in the office. Of course, I was grimly wrong. Anyone in a small office (or large one, for that matter) who has ever covered for someone who is on vacation knows that it is usually twice the work load to assume. And, in my case, since I was covering for two absent bosses and trying to keep a business running, it felt even harder. The phones showed me no mercy during this vacation—I was constantly trying to retrace my bosses' steps and cover their tracks—they had left me a list of clients who they did not want to know they were out of town. For two days I said that my bosses were at meetings, or at a rehearsal, backstage in a dressing room or not back from lunch. I hated lying. I wasn't a very good actor, though I had managed to fend off Jerome Robbins and Bobby Short, among others, set up an interview with an actor and the *Daily News*, and help an out-of-town critic get press tickets. One small-time producer, however, wasn't buying my lie and demanded to speak with my boss. After his third or fourth phone call to the office, when he stopped short of calling me an ugly name, I called the number of the coast guard that I had been given to use only for emergencies and was patched through to the phone aboard the ship. A man who I assumed was the captain answered the line and I asked to speak with my boss (the butch one). While I waited for her to come to the phone, another man came on the line and asked, "What's the weather like in New York?" It was unmistakably Rock Hudson. "Cold and stormy," I answered, wondering if he was aware that I was also talking in metaphors. "Well, let's hope it clears up before these two try to catch a flight home."

The next thing I knew my boss was on the line. She was not in a good mood. I had obviously disturbed her for unimportant business. When I told her about the continuous calls from the producer, she let out a string of expletives. She sounded a bit drunk, but then she wanted to know everyone who had called the office while she was away. I went down the list I had been collecting. When I reached Jerome Robbins, she interrupted me and said in her little girl voice, "Jerry called? When did Jerry call?"

After I had given her an answer and the phone number Jerome Robbins had left, she reverted to the booming voice of an ogre that I had come to expect and received a dressing down because I should have known to call her about Jerome Robbins and not the small time producer.

As I moved through the remainder of the week with a frantic skill, it occurred to me that I had to find a way out of this "career" and change the direction of my life if I wanted to become a writer. Here I was in my mid-twenties, already facing a midlife crisis.

During the second year of my apprenticeship, a small story was published on the back page of the first section of *The New York Times*. It was a news report about a type of cancer which was being found in gay men. I remember that it triggered a lot of thoughts and questions within me, foremost the notion if my desire to have sex with a man instead of a woman was biologically determined. At this point my story takes a similar route of other gay men in the city during those days. We worried, we read the news, we talked with friends and compared potential symptoms and confusions over the concept of "safe sex." The theater community was one of the first and hardest hit by the first wave of the AIDS epidemic. I worked or attended early fundraisers at cabarets, discos, art galleries, theaters, and even a performance of the circus. I can remember when the phone would ring in the office and the conversation would be over a sudden change in casting because an actor was in the hospital or gossip about whether a certain director or producer might be ill. And many of these remarks were about people I knew and worked with on a daily basis.

The analogies that have compared the early years of the AIDS epidemic to trying to survive in a war zone were apt. Some days I felt it impossible to control the direction of my life because each piece of news that arrived was like another bomb exploding. And, as the truth became more grim, I carried around a depression that was difficult to shake off.

As it happened, the years passed and I completed my three-year apprenticeship, and, not long afterward, I held a union contract for the office for the national tour of a play. While this new position allowed me some opportunity to travel to other cities and be outside of the office for days at a time, it did not remove any stress I felt from the job nor did it change my dislike for the profession of being a publicist. My bosses had also reached a change in their own thinking about my role in the office; they now expected me to bring in new clients, something that they had clearly not championed during my prior years nor had even bothered to discuss with me. When the national tour suddenly closed due to a lack of sales, I found myself back in New York and without a job because the office was without enough clients to support paying all three of us salaries. Within days, however, I was fortunate enough to find a job in the corporate sector helping publicize, among other things, spray paint, motor oil, and fast-food hamburgers. This was another odd fit for me, and when, a few weeks later, another theatrical contract was offered to me in a different (though still small) entertainment publicity firm, I returned because I had not found a sense of self-confidence in any other place besides the theater. This, too, was another unfortunate decision for me to make; I went to work for a man I had known socially through my theater friends only to find out that he maintained a nervous, hyper-officious alter ego in the office. He made the butch and femme look like school girls.

Throughout all this I did not lose my desire to be a writer. I had long since finished the itinerant actor-musician novel, sent it out directly to a list of editors and publishers I had culled from press clippings, and had a large folder of rejection letters that did not so much disappoint me as challenged me to become a better writer. And so my life in the city became a daily routine of odd contrasts, walking uptown to Times Square from my office near Macy's, for instance, to cover an interview in a young Alec Baldwin's dressing room, only to leave a few minutes later so I could sit in a small neighborhood park in Hell's Kitchen and read a book that I hoped held some new clue for me on how to be a better writer, before the next duty at the theater called me back to Broadway, or the sun set and I was forced to return to my tiny, expensive apartment. I refused to allow these two personas to overlap though it was often hard to keep them separate. I told very few people about my writing because I was afraid of being mocked and losing my passion to continue. And I was continuing to write about working in the theater, but now my stories were closer to my own experiences. I had written a short story about an actor who was trying to hide his illness, loosely based on a client I had known while I worked in the publicity office. I knew it wasn't ready to be published, so I enrolled in a writing workshop that was being held on the Upper West Side, hoping to find a way to make it better.

This was the point I was at when the news of Rock Hudson's death came to me. It wasn't difficult to glance back and remember when I met him at the opening night party or talked with him during his Caribbean vacation with my former bosses. It almost seemed like an idyllic time in my mind; since then, the ground beneath me had shifted and trembled with and without my own uncertain steps. In the wake of Hudson's death, the media would begin to change their coverage of AIDS. Elizabeth Taylor, his longtime friend, shocked that no one even wanted to mention the word, went into action and helped form The American Foundation for AIDS Research, at a time when then-President Reagan steadfastly refused to even acknowledge the crisis.

And in truth, I believe that Rock Hudson's death did not change anything in my life that was not already on that course before it happened. But it did make me realize that what had been a part of my former job in the theater was not necessarily going to be a part of my future years in the city as a would-be writer. I never really lost my love of the theater, but during these early years of the epidemic, it just grew into a smaller and less important part of myself. AIDS would further impact me in ways that I could never imagine. It would take me a few more personal crises to find my own voice on the page and the way to the stories I felt I should tell. But one other thing that became resolutely clear to me at this moment: There was no going back to what had once been—things had changed and I had to find a new way to survive.

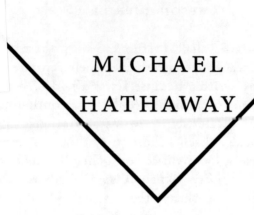

MICHAEL HATHAWAY

CHIRON REVIEW

MICHAEL HATHAWAY founded *Chiron Review* literary journal in 1982 and has had twelve books of poetry and prose published. He's published 300+ poems and creative nonfictions in journals and anthologies including *The James White Review*; *Van Gogh's Ear*; *A Day for a Lay: A Century of Gay Poetry*; *Walking Higher: Gay Men Write About the Deaths of Their Mothers*; and *Obsessed: A Flesh and the Word Collection of Gay Erotic Memoirs*. He lives in St. John, Kansas, with his feline family and has worked as Keeper of History for Stafford County since 2000. He also works part-time for his veterinarian for the employee discounts. For more about *Chiron Review*, visit www.chironreview.com.

Q: What is the last thing a poet taught you?

The last thing a poet [Catherine Lynn] taught me was that "less is more." As poets, it's important to move past the idea that every word we commit to paper (or computer screen) is a masterpiece. Be economical with words; make every word count. Edit and proofread carefully. Don't get in a hurry. Walk away from it and let a poem "simmer" for a couple (or few) weeks. Then take a fresh look at it, read it aloud, and make any needed corrections or improvements before sending it out into the world.

MICHAEL HATHAWAY

TWENTY YEARS OF *CHIRON REVIEW*

This essay, originally published in Chiron Review #68 *in 2002, celebrated the 20th anniversary of the literary magazine.*

I started the magazine with no intention of spending my whole life at it. I intended to publish until age 30, then devote the rest of my life to some job working with and taking care of animals. Well, 30 came and went, now 40 has come and gone, and here I still am. But since there has been a parade of stray cats through my life and every house I've ever lived in has unofficially been a home for abandoned cats, I guess in a way I've fulfilled that goal as well. At this writing I live with a house full of fuzzy varmints and take care of others who don't live with me.

I was a month away from my 20th birthday when I began typesetting the first issue in August 1981. This was done on now-antique typesetting machines in the composing room where I worked as typesetter at the *Great Bend* [Kansas] *Daily Tribune*. The issue was typeset on a machine that punched holes in one-inch paper tape. Each letter, digit, and command had its own combination of holes, up to six in the line. This computer had no screen or mouse. The operators of these machines could not see what they had typed. In order to make corrections, the operator translated the series of holes, "erased" (reversing the tape and blacking out the errors with all six holes), and then re-typed the copy correctly. This sounds scary in these days of giant monitors and mice, but I was good at it, and my boss told me I typed the cleanest copy he'd ever seen since he started in 1961 (126 wpm, 99.4% accuracy).

The paper tape was run through a monstrous computer. Fonts were on two long, changeable filmstrips that were attached to a wheel inside the computer. The wheel spun very fast as it "read" the paper tape and shot appropriate characters onto paper film. The film was taken to the dark room and developed. Then it was trimmed, waxed, and pasted up on the page. Further line corrections could be made and pasted up after the copy was on the page. Typesetting was no problem. For some reason, it took five months to paste up the eight-page premier issue, featuring cousin Connie Edwards, double-cousin Karen Hathaway, best friend Richard Fisher, a classmate, several pen pals, and mom. (I can't for the life of me remember why it took so long to finish such a small issue. Now I whip out a 48-page issue, typos and all, in three to four weeks.) I pasted up that first issue at a small round kitchen table in my trailer at 808 Maple, with curious cats lolling about on the pages, batting playful paws at my trusty X-Acto knife, pica pole, and indelible blue pen.

Titled *The Kindred Spirit* (a phrase from *Anne of Green Gables* by L.M. Montgomery), it was published February 19, 1982. It was here I learned the act of creation packed a more powerful rush than any drug or drink. I was hooked for life. The first three copies were sold literally hot off the press to newspaper co-workers for 50¢. I was astonished and delighted that anyone would give me money for it. The first several issues weren't much to brag about. In 1987, I met Jay Dougherty who began, through a flurry of patient correspondence, guiding me step-by-step into improving the magazine's content (and how, when, and why to say no to submissions).

In 1989, Gerald Locklin agreed to become poetry editor and Ray Zepeda agreed to become fiction editor. The magazine changed from *The Kindred Spirit* to *Chiron Review* as of Issue 18, Spring, 1989. Thanks to their guidance, *Chiron Review* became, among other things, a small "outpost" of a refreshing movement in American literature. Charles Harper Webb calls it Stand-Up; Ed Ochester calls it Neo-Populist. Whatever it is, it's an unpretentious literature that is accessible beyond the ivory towers of academia and outside the bounds of religious or politically-correct restrictions. It celebrates honesty and humor. It also reclaims poetry as an art for the so-called "common" people. It seemed like something worthwhile to which to dedicate my life.

In spite of this, *Chiron Review* has fought an on-going battle with hostility and attempted censorship—some silent, some blatant. (I use the term "censorship" here to mean any stifling of free speech and freedom of the press. Gerry Locklin gently pointed out that "censorship" in the truest definition of the word can only be committed by a government, not an individual or private business. I couldn't find a word that means the same fascist crap being pulled by someone who isn't a government, someone legally superimposing his own inalienable rights over someone else's, so I took liberties.)

Nothing serious came of any attempts to stifle *Chiron Review*, though they seemed serious when they were happening. I'm well aware that many writers and publishers in the US and in other parts of the world have sacrificed their freedom, well-being, and too often their very lives for expressing themselves freely. Regardless of the intensity of oppression, stifling of self-expression in any form in the US is a slap in the face to human rights and to our forefathers and foremothers who sacrificed and died for the basic freedoms our country is based on. There's no challenge or soul-searching in cheering for people we agree with or championing free speech for people who are saying what we want to hear. Freedom becomes most meaningful, defined in its purest, most honest form when we defend freedom of speech and pursuit of life, liberty, and happiness for someone we dislike, disapprove of, or disagree with.

I've always maintained that *Chiron Review* is not political and has no specific agenda, but that's not entirely true. The act of creating *Chiron Review* is political. Stubbornly continuing to publish whatever I choose to publish has become an aggressive political act—nothing short of a holy war. The urge to fight, to preserve this right and freedom by continuing to do it without compromise is as political as it gets. It will sound trite and simple-minded, but it's all about freedom. What it boils down to is that I publish each issue with eternal optimism, with the never-ending hope readers will not only be entertained, educated, and enlightened by the literary offerings, but understand that to be truly free, we must allow others to be free, in their own way, on their own terms. There is no reason to make things any more complicated than that.

Every issue of *Chiron Review* features poems and stories which challenge readers to the very limit in the tolerance arena. Most readers celebrate this challenge, but others cave to their baser instincts to annihilate all who dare to offend or disagree with them or rattle the foundations of their belief systems. *Chiron Review* writers won't shy away from the controversial. They meet difficult and inflammatory subjects head-on, with style, grace, and most of all, honesty—sometimes, brutal honesty. There is no word or subject that is unspeakable or so dangerous it can't be uttered. Writers who use language or subject matter simply for the sake of shock are boring. At the same time, I have great respect for a writer that doesn't practice self-censorship for public approval (or any other reason), that doesn't shy away from radical philosophy, politically explosive, or sexually-explicit subject matter or coarse language when the story requires one or all of those ingredients. These are legitimate aspects of the rich, colorful tapestry of our lives, and I don't believe in sweeping them under the carpet. I don't believe in sanitizing truth for public consumption. I don't believe in pussyfooting around the delicate sensibilities of squeamish, weak-minded people.

I've noticed those readers with delicate sensibilities and intolerant, overly-moralistic religious views tend to look for and comment on only what offends them. Ironically, much of the subject matter and writing in *Chiron Review* is quite tame, but I'm still waiting for some Christian or Republican to walk up to me on the street, pat me on the back, and congratulate me for that. I continue to assert the biggest challenge to sensitive readers is to keep reading, once they've started an issue, regardless of personal views. The biggest challenge is to find tolerance for what is different or foreign to his/her own mind-set, to find something to celebrate and love, not rage against what s/he hates. The challenge is to find the common thread that makes us all human.

Through my day-job as curator and librarian of our local historical museum, my passion for genealogy was rekindled. I learned my great-great-great-grandfather John Fitzgerald immigrated from England via Ireland to become an original settler of Stafford County, Kansas, where I live. My great-great-grandfather John Henry (Jack) Hathaway and two of his sons participated in the Cherokee Strip Land Run. Great-grandfather Walter Smith, Sr., participated in the Land Run and was an original settler of Cowley County, Kansas (where *Chiron Review* was once printed). Great-grandfather Charles Griffin and grandfather Ezra Smith, Sr., homesteaded in Montana in the early 1900's. Mom's ancestors on her father's side go back to "original patriots" who came over on the Mayflower and sister ships.

I mention my forefathers not to assume honor by association or heredity or to rest on their laurels, but to suggest maybe their hearty, undaunted pioneer spirit is alive and well, still manifesting and celebrating itself on the plains of Kansas in the pages of *Chiron Review*.

That's not to say some of the content of *Chiron Review* wouldn't curl their hair were they alive today, that all my venerable forefathers wouldn't be walking around with chronic curly perms . . . but I see *Chiron* writers as true pioneers—brave rebels and righteous outlaws. They break rules and do things frightened, uptight, rigid, little-minded people say can't or shouldn't be done in writing. They strive constantly for liberation. Our writers continually break new ground. Not literally on the harsh, unforgiving Kansas prairie as my ancestors did, but on an always new and changing frontier: the landscape of the human heart, experience, and self-expression; a landscape that can be just as rugged, unforgiving, and fraught with one looming, dangerous obstacle after another.

Chiron Review #68 will mark, for better or worse, the accomplishment of the first 40 years of my life. I'm proud of this milestone, of the magazine; proud we have overcome many obstacles and are still alive and kicking literary ass, not much the worse for wear. A high school teacher told one of my cousins she wishes I'd "gone to college and done something" with my life and talents. I had been blissfully oblivious that I hadn't "done anything" with my life. I suppose I could have done more, but still can't muster up any regret.

Regardless of my lack of education and of having never gone to college, I still managed to stumble headlong into something so utterly real, something beyond academia, beyond intellectual, beyond spiritual—a calling and vocation so perfect they could not have been planned. This life's work I stumbled into is one I've been able to "learn by doing" with guidance from accomplished poets and editors in the business. There might not be a better classroom in the world. I am grateful for this education and wouldn't trade it for any college degree. I'm honored and humbled to be the publisher of so many brilliant writers and to be the one who presents their beatific creations to the world (even though only a handful of people are listening). It remains the most sacred of tasks to publish a literary journal that brings such wild masterpieces to the light of day. It remains, after 20 years, the reason I get out of bed each day.

LETTER TO BILLY T., 1985

The mailman brought you into my life
with your poems of isolation, pain and damnation.
I can't bear to know you are giving up.
I have to let you know I care,
a face I've never seen, a voice I've never heard,
a lonely boy surrounded by thick darkness,
crying out through your typewriter
your sad songs.

Hold on sweet boy, hold on—
There will always be love living here for you.
There is always love.
You must never give in to the harsh winds of hate,
not when love will burn for you so strong,
so loud, so hot.

AS IF I DIDN'T HAVE ENOUGH POETS
CRAWLING OUT OF THE WOODWORK

I've taken to naming cats
after poets.

So far there's shy, reclusive
Emily Dickinson,
tone deaf Stevie Nicks,
"Annie" Sexton, who has used up
more than her share of lives,

and the newest addition,
Sylvia, a kitten
who spends most of her time
trying to figure out a way
to get into the oven.

A BOY & SOME BULLIES

He goes for an evening walk
to be with wind and stars and moon.
The bullies don't approve
of how he walks or
how his long hair
dances with the wind.
They drive by mocking,
taunting, yelling,
FAGGOTMOTHERFUCKER!
The boy ignores them,
keeps walking.
The bullies drive on deeper
into their darkness.

THE LAST POEM
FOR TRACY

I offerered life
scented as morning coffee,
alfalfa in bloom,
poetry at midnight,
roses, lilacs,
the very singing heart
of springtime.

He grunted, puked,
rolled joints in pages
bleeding holy poetry,
stole cars, guns,
craved cheap cigarettes,
stale beer,
and 3 AM whores in heat.

WILLIAM JOHNSON

LAMBDA LITERARY

&

MARY LITERARY

WILLIAM JOHNSON is the online editor of *Lambda Literary*. He is also the editor and publisher of *Mary Literary*, a journal dedicated to publishing gay writing of artistic merit, and a contributing arts and culture writer for *CRUSHfanzine*.

Q: Who, writing now, excites you?

Writer/Musician Brontez Purnell is currently one of my favorite writers. His writing is visceral, unfiltered, and funny. His topics include "semen addiction" and twerking to Too $hort. I love him.

Q: What is the publisher's greatest responsibility?

To publish work that changes/upsets the gravitational pull of the world.

SPEAKING CAMP

"It was huge. It looked like a giant black silo," he sighed. "A baby's arm holding a plum. It looked like an eggplant. A huge zucchini."

My friend T and I are talking on the phone about a late night rendezvous he'd had the night before.

"It was massive. I did not know if I should've sucked this guy's dick or given it an area code," he said. "I was literally stunned into silence."

"You without words?" I said.

"It was only a momentary loss of reason," T continued, "but I rose up. I met the challenge. Like Moses, I climbed the mountaintop."

"To seek the face of God?" I asked.

"In a matter of speaking, yes. Now after my sodomy-filled sojourn I have come back to spread the holy glory!"

"Praise be," I said.

"Hallelujah!" he said.

"When I was younger I wanted love and companionship. I wanted romance and roses. Champagne and Cole Porter love songs. I was much younger then."

"And now?"

"I'll just take the dick."

"Apparently," I said.

★

Camp. This is language I often speak, and this is the language I love. If the Blues is the one truly American art form, then the Camp aesthetic is the truly homosexual one. The Camp aesthetic flamboyantly seizes on standard cultural norms, entities, or expressions, does a very finely tuned assessment of those normative ideals, and then repositions them humorously through a sissified lens. Camp basically turns straight "things" into faggy "things."

Camp is irony's limp-wristed little sister. It uses a gay aesthetic to turn the "proper" inside out.

In her famous essay, "Notes on Camp," Susan Sontag deftly touched on some of the key tenets of Camp. "The whole point of Camp," she wrote, "is to dethrone the serious. Camp is playful, anti-serious. More precisely, Camp involves a new, more complex relation to 'the serious.'"

When a gay artist employs Camp purposely to express high-minded ideals it makes my mind leap and my heart explode with happiness. It combines my love for "feeling" and "thought" with my fondness of uprooting bogus conceits.

There is a genius in not letting the satirical voice extinguish actual feeling. I'm thinking Andrew Holleran, Morrissey, Justin Bond, Kalup Linzy . . . gay artists/performers who employ the "camp voice" not only to remix and reexamine the absurdity of the "sincere straight" narrative, but also to use camp as a means to get at something deeper about the human condition. They are both campy and sincere at the same time. To me this is an incredible hat trick. When talking with Justin Bond about the subject recently, he had this to say:

> I don't think sincerity and irony are mutually exclusive, because the world is so absurd. I do think there is a way that you can express yourself with general emotion and at the same time be fully aware of the absurdity of those emotions. So I think in life sincerity and irony are often not mutually exclusive at all.

★

As he waited on the sidewalk beneath us for a client to arrive, a beggar approached Sutherland and held out his hand and said: "I'm hungry." And Sutherland said to him, with that suppressed hysteria that lurked behind his breathless voice: "I'm hungry too, for love, self-esteem, and religious certainty. You are merely hungry for food." And he gave the man a Valium.

- Dancer from the Dance
Andrew Holleran 1978

★

I am trying to remember the first time I spoke in a camp voice. Other things in gay life are easier to catalogue: the first crush, the first kiss, the first person you came out to. But when was the first time you did something campy? In 1985, I was thirteen years old. To pass the time my friends and I would sit in my room and record silly skits on my bright red Sony tape recorder. The skits we created were always juvenile spoofs of popular TV shows of the time (i.e. Scooby-Doo became Scooby-Poo, a farting, crime-solving dog).

One rainy afternoon I taped a thirty minute skit spoofing the popular cartoon-cum-girl-band melodrama *Jem and The Holograms*. Jem was an animated show that revolved around an all-girl band and their constant struggle to use their musical careers to fund a good natured foster home for girls called the Starlight House. In my skit I renamed the show's characters, making all their names derivative of anything associated with jelly or canned preservatives. Jem and The Holograms became Jam and The Jellys. In the skit, the characters, instead of having hot 80's monikers like Jerrica, Rio, and Kimber, were renamed Grape, Cherry, and Marmalade. I renamed the bratty villains of the show, the nefarious girl band The Misfits, The Smuckers. In this improvised skit I basically recreated the cartoon's histrionic plot lines, but by renaming the characters it gave the whole proceedings a silly, surreal edge that amused our adolescent sensibilities.

"Oh, Marmalade! What if Grape doesn't call me back for a second date?" I asked into the tape recorder with a girlish lilt. I even sang a revised version of the iconic Jem theme sing: "Jam is truly delicious. Truly, truly delicious. Ohhhhh Jam!" My voice rose in an off-key falsetto. "Jam is my name; tasty, delicious biscuits are my game! Jam!"

I had my friends sing the Misfit's hard rocker chick chorus with reworked jelly-inspired lyrics: "We are the Smuckers! We are the Smuckers! Our songs are better. We are going get her. We're gonna. We're gonna get her!"

★

I am so clever that sometimes I don't understand a single word of what I am saying.

- "The Remarkable Rocket"
Oscar Wilde 1888

ASSARACUS   141

★

The Oxford English Dictionary describes the Camp aesthetic as "ostentatious, exaggerated, affected, theatrical; effeminate or homosexual. . . ."

To which T says, "Sounds like the Equinox Gym on Greenwich Street on a Wednesday night."

★

In college, I staged a comedic play where Moby Dick and Ahab meet-cute on an episode of *The Love Boat*. I played Julie, the cruise director.

★

Camp is the voice of the aesthetically anarchic. If there is a tangible boundary, a recognizable signpost for cultural normalcy and decency, there will be some homosexual elegantly sucking a cock right on top of it.

★

T says when Teena Marie hits that shockingly high note in the middle of her song "Portuguese Love," it sounds like "someone just placed a dollop of cold ice cream on her vagina."

★

In high school I sat in my room and listened to The Smiths constantly. I made depressive mixtapes for all my friends. "Girlfriend in a Coma" was always one of the songs that I predominantly featured on the various compilations I created. This song really spoke to me. It was only years later, when my homosexuality truly reared its man-on-man loving head, that I realized why.

★

It was not a good day for the young actor. He had been having trouble

with the director all day.
"You're not photographing me with my best side to the camera"
he complained.
"But how can I tell?" the director rejoined acidly. "You're sitting
on it."

- "Jokes Worth Repeating"
David Magazine Spring 1972

★

Camp is often a revolutionary tool used to usurp counterfeit ideals.
But it does so with jokes. It is not often that a revolution can have
jokes.

★

When I was in my twenties I was obsessed with the Joan Crawford bio
picture *Mommie Dearest*. The general consensus is that Faye Dunaway's
brutal, over-the-top portrayal of Joan Crawford ruined Dunaway's
career, but I think she is brilliant in the movie. She shrewdly "acts"
like a woman who can't stop acting. It's a performance on top of a
performance, an uncanny hall of mirrors. She is ridiculing artifice by
being artificial.

★

T has nick-named his anus. He calls it his "little magical pussy." When
he walks by a hot straight guy on the street he often farts loudly and
then whispers to me, "I bet his girlfriend's pussy can't do that. *My
pussy can whistle.*"

★

I understand one can't live off Camp alone. Too much of it is like
eating five vanilla éclairs in a row. Too much richness can make
you sick. When my friends and I kiki too much, I become mentally
exhausted. All that repartee is draining. When this happens I call my
mother. She is the one thing I love that is the opposite of Camp. She

is good natured. She talks about her garden and making salmon for dinner. My conversations with my mother clear my head of all that faggoty clutter. When we are done talking I almost always pick up the phone right after to call my dear friend T. T and I have a conversation that inevitably turns to how "Miss Oprah's weaves are so immense they must draw their own salary and health benefits from Harpo's production company." Balance is important. You must learn not to revolt against feelings that are true. Genuineness is not the true enemy of Camp; insincerity posing as honesty is.

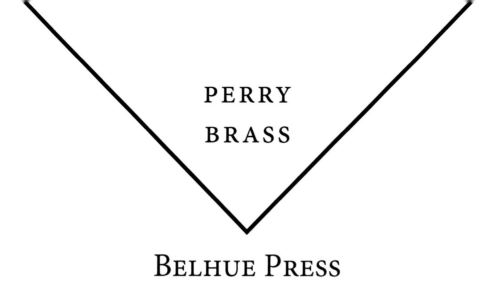

PERRY BRASS

BELHUE PRESS

PERRY BRASS has published sixteen books through Belhue Press, including the best-selling *The Manly Art of Seduction*, which starts off with the assumption that "men are not supposed to be seductive," which of course is all the fun of being it. Also of note is *King of Angels*, a gay Southern Jewish coming-of-age novel set in his native Savannah in 1963, the year of J.F.K's assassination. Perry has been a finalist six times for Lambda Literary Awards, won four IPPY Awards from Jenkins Group Publishing Services, won a Rainbow Award, and with *King of Angels*, was named a finalist for a 2013 Ferro-Grumley Award for LGBT fiction. You can learn more about Perry at his website, www.perrybrass.com, or you can reach him through Facebook.

Q: What is the role of poetry in today's queer landscape?

The role of poetry in today's queer landscape should be what it probably has always been: to tell the truth that most people have a hard time telling and hearing, and also to turn around and expand consciousness using the tool of language. Poetry does that very well. Poetry has always had a large queer presence in it, so our place in it is pretty much established. What is missing now is the audience for it—I remember when gay poetry readings attracted hundreds of people; I wish that were still the case.

NINE LIFE LESSONS IN BOOK PUBLISHING

I was very fortunate when I first started putting out books, in 1990, under the imprint Belhue Press, named for my sister, Nancy Belle Howard, and my partner (and now husband), Hugh Young. The idea of gay books then as a separate category of books was gaining some grudging respect in the general book trade. That is, there was some acceptance of queer material, although it was still pretty much an underground market, and despite the emergence of gay bookstores in a few key cities, like New York, San Francisco, Boston, and Los Angeles, most of the mainstream book world (publishers, distributors, marketers, and publicists) still turned its back on them. This meant that the audience for queer books was actually more receptive to new ideas and materials than the market was giving them; in fact, the audience was hungry for them.

Like a lot of writers, I began to self–publish because I could not get any traction from standard publishers, and even, frankly, the few queer ones were still stuck in very narrow ruts, usually streaked with heavy glops of internalized homophobia. I was a poet from a politically-radical, gay background who basically could not be published in mainstream publications because my work was too overtly "gay." Neither was I part of the more conservative fashions on display at the time in what passed for gay literature. In short, I had a "following," but it was very, *very* small. I'd been writing and even occasionally publishing my literary work for almost twenty years, but I'd also been freelancing commercial writing for fifteen, which gave me an idea of how publishing worked from the standpoint of a freelancer, but no grasp at all of how book publishing operated.

Then—*eureka!*—I had an idea which I thought was truly novel: I'd publish a book of my sexually unabashed poetry illustrated by the kind of gorgeous, male photography then jumping into the market after Robert Mapplethorpe's big-splash, popular success. I became friends with John Wessel, part owner of Wessel+O'Connor Gallery, a very successful, ultra-hip photo gallery on lower Broadway in New York. I approached John with my idea; he was very supportive. Quickly I queried five or six gay publishers, and found everyone of them completely deaf to my idea. Like a lot of writers, I had become used to rejection slips, but this concept seemed very commercially flyable. Gay photography was leaping off the walls, and I knew at this point probably six photographers I could approach with Wessel's help. I went from being dejected to angry, and decided, like Mickey Rooney in too many Judy Garland movies, to put the show on myself.

I already had the idea for the name of my press, and quickly called everyone I knew who could be of any help to me, including, first, a lawyer. He told me that to set up a business and make it, henceforth and forever more, legally foolproof would cost me around $7,000 in legal fees. I hung up the phone.

Lesson Number One: Don't pay lawyers unless you absolutely have to. (I haven't.)

I also called up a successful writer friend who'd likewise been a publisher and told him that I wanted to call my first book *Sex-charge*. He advised me: "I like the idea, but, whatever you do, *don't* put a hot cover on it. You'll never be taken seriously as a poet, and it won't sell."

Again I hung up the phone.

Lesson Number Two: Don't take everyone's advice.

Au contraire, I'd already made my mind that I wanted the cover of my book to be so hot it'd curl the page. With John Wessel's help, I got an incendiary cover shot from Joe Ziolkowski, a gifted young photographer whose work had not been yet showcased in a book. For a small fee, I got Joe's cover photo, as well as several other black and white shots of comely young naked men to be catnip inside the book.

Now I had to find a printer. I'd been warned that a lot of book printers would not go near me because they were scared their other customers might pop into the shop, see my covers, and pee all over themselves from fear or fury. My author-publisher friend suggested I go to a print jobber, that is someone who assembles print jobs for smaller printers operating without a sales rep. Bait: I would get a great deal! I had a meeting with a jobber who presented me with a basic fact: *the more books you print, the less they cost.* "If you do 3,000 copies," he revealed, like Houdini, "you can do this book for about . . . 68¢ per copy."

OMG! With that kind of cost *per* book, at a retail of $6.95, I *had* to make money. We shook hands, and I noticed him smiling and kind of winking at me. Later on, I understood why. Nobody in his right mind would print *3,000* copies of a maiden voyage book of poetry by an almost unknown writer. About four months later, *Sex-charge* came back from the printer. I was buzzing with excitement. Hugh and I were living in a converted farmhouse in rural Connecticut with a basement large enough to store 3,000 copies of my slim 78-page book. I fell asleep that night happier than I could ever remember being: there below us was my first book. In all those sealed boxes. It was like they were all talking to me, and guess what they were saying?

"Now you've got to SELL us!"

I'd prepared a single-page sales sheet about *Sex-charge*, spotlighting the cover. I grabbed a copy of the venerable old *Gay Yellow Pages*, and phoned every bookstore and gift shop listed, then mailed out the sales sheets. Quickly—lo and behold—just what I'd hoped to happen did: my cover sold the book. People who'd never heard of me wanted it. They also loved the overtness of the title, and that while a lot of the poems were funny as well as sexy, just as many were also dead-on serious—after all, men were still dying of AIDS everyday.

A couple of my writer friends with books out said: "It's time to look for a distributor."

A *what*? I had no idea what a distributor did, much less how to get one—but I was also told, "It's important a distributor does *not* know that you, the writer of the book, is also the publisher."

I snared a list of distributors, called up three or four of them and informed them I was "Hugh, of Bel-*hue* Press, publisher of a new line of books out of Connecticut, with a great new book of poetry called *Sex-charge*." My second conversation was with a young man named Ron Hanby at Golden-Lee, a company that distributed the ever-popular line of Little Golden children's books but was also trying to crack the emerging gay book market. Ron was a wrestling enthusiast (okay, fetishist), and as I told him about *Sex-charge*, he started salivating on the phone. He immediately signed me, and I decided, screw it: I could be *Perry Brass* with Ron. I could not, though, with bigger distributors. With them, I needed to be more deadpan "businesslike" than writers are given credit for being. Using my "Hugh, the publisher" persona, we were also signed by Inland Book Company, also in Connecticut, the largest distributor of independent press books on the East Coast.

Lesson Number Three: Like Tom Terrific, initially you can be what you *want* to be—then later develop into the larger person necessary to be your own *real* self.

By now, *Sex-charge* was selling like hot cakes. My friend, the writer T.R. Witomski ("America's leading writer of S&M porn stories"), decided to put out a catalogue offering everything for the young man of kink, bondage, and other allied tastes. In it, along with movies, enema equipment, and dildos, he included *Sex-charge*: "Entertaining and often filthy. Poetry for people who don't like poetry."

We were now burning merrily through the 3,000 copies.

Lesson Number Four: Don't just think outside the box. Destroy the box.

Yes, I now had to start thinking more like a publisher and less like a poet. I was giving dozens of readings from the book, something I'd been way too shy to do before, and I started to understand something: people—the *audience*—loved what I was doing. They were connecting with my work and with me. That was what I'd been wanting; the queer literati could go *Sex-charge* themselves!

A few months after my poetry book came out, three things happened that seemed like amazing gifts of fortune. First, like a bolt out the sky, I knew what my next book would be. It just landed on me simple as that. I had no interest in science fiction, but I'd had a very strange, twisted dream while staying in Washington, D.C.

Washington, I'd known for years, was a very temporary city for "of-the-moment" people. It would be easy to fall into it, assume a completely new identity, and then get the hell out. My dream was about two men who did such a thing. I awoke from it with a start. My question was: Who were they and what were they actually *capable* of doing? As this dream turned into a book, I thought: Suppose these two men had fallen into Washington from another planet? And suppose they were a gay couple, one of them an articulate and sensitive youth but insecure about his looks as young people are, and the other an impetuous, sexually-rife older guy, fully capable of murder?

I was riding through Connecticut when the title and plot for *Mirage* roared into me. I wasn't even creating it; as a writer, it was creating *me*. A few weeks later, I was at a copy shop a few miles from our house when I noticed a young woman with long, streaky blonde hair working on her design portfolio. I asked her if I could take a look, then asked her if she ever designed books.

She told me that she had designed brochures for CBS and would love a chance to design books. Her name was Mimi Fitzhugh; she came to my house a few days later, and we began a collaboration that would last through twelve books until Mimi decided to leave graphic design. Mimi was about twelve years younger than I, and a driving perfectionist. We were both Virgos and got along perfectly. As a designer, and often a proofreader and my assistant, she spotted places where I screwed up, thought about things that never occurred to me, and had no qualms about working on material that could have gotten both of us put up against a wall and shot in some countries.

The third luck came when I was leafing through an old *Christopher Street* magazine. I spotted a layout of photos by a young photographer of Portuguese extraction living in Montreal named Gilberto Prioste. His work had a raw, animal intensity; I called *Christopher Street* and got his phone number. He sent me a selection of his work, and I picked one for the cover of *Mirage*. I now had a title, a concept, a cover, but no book.

As I learned later on, that was enough.

Lesson Number Five: Always be on the look out for talent—for people who can make a big difference in your life. You can find them at a copy shop, over coffee, or in the pages of an old magazine.

And Lesson Number Six: The right idea is everything. Run with it, develop it, and work it hard, so it becomes your own.

I decided to get a publicist. I'd met Michele Karlsberg when she worked at Mavety Media Works, a mega-publisher of gay erotica that had a tendency to hire extraordinary people. Michele had been assistant to an editor I worked with there. She decided to go out on her own, and I was her first client. She immediately suggested we bring *Mirage*, which still only existed as a one-page sales sheet with a picture of Mimi's cover design on it, to the American Booksellers Association convention at the Javits Center in New York. I was extremely nervous; I'd have to appear as the author and publisher of a book I hadn't even written yet, jumping directly into the sharky, big-money world of publishing. Michele held my hand as we walked into the Javits Center. She quickly introduced me to dozens of people who took one look at my sales sheet and freaked out.

There it was: a totally *queer*, hyper-erotically-charged science fiction novel with two guys on the cover who looked like they were ready to devour each other whole. Two distributors started fighting over who would get to distribute *Mirage* in England; media people flocked to me. Bookstores came up to me and said they'd sold *Sex-charge* and couldn't wait to get their mits on *Mirage*. I went home so excited I could barely sleep. Michele got me connected to a printer in Michigan who took on the book without blinking over the "subject matter." I spent the next six months drowning in work, learning how to use a brand new Mac "classic" with a screen as big as a postcard to get the book completed. I also hired someone to proofread the book, who also came out of Mavety, and spent a whole hundred bucks to pay him.

Lesson Number Seven: Spend more money on talent. Try to exceed yourself in professionalism. I needed more than a proofreader; I needed a really good editor. But I wouldn't get one for the next several books.

Mirage took off fast. Barnes and Noble declared it one of "100 Hot Books to Look Out For." The characters in it became the basis for my trilogy of gay science fiction novels dealing with the men and women of Ki, a distant small planet where population control is important and keeping the "balance of the planet" paramount. (All of this a full decade before the global warming threat really emerged.) The head of Inland Books, David Wilk, phoned "Hugh" and asked if *Mirage* had become a course requirement in any colleges. I told him not as far as I knew. He was puzzled, and added, "Books like this, from really small presses, never sell in *these* numbers unless they do."

What had happened was in fact different. *Mirage* had presented a completely unique gay character in Greeland, the hunter from Ki: a brazenly sexual, passionate, unpredictable, and attractive guy who was 100% *male*. For me Greeland was not a fantasy, but a reality; I'd known several real Greelands in my life. He was the polar opposite of the simpy, wounded, viperish *Dancer from the Dance* queers then dominating gay lit. His relationship with the younger Albert delighted people. One reader gushed to me, "If Albert doesn't want Greeland, *I* do."

But a lot of people in the gay science fiction world did *not* want him. The fact that I was an openly gay, Jewish storyteller (and poet) and not a science fiction writer distanced me from that audience. I was invited to several Gaylaxicons, the yearly queer science fiction get-together, and at first liked them. Then I realized something: Gaylaxicon attendees were not interested in creating a new queer science fiction culture; they were bent on injecting a couple of gay characters into old franchises, like *Star Wars*. By my third Gaylaxicon I saw that I was the only openly gay male writer there (although they usually had a few openly lesbian ones). I was actively snubbed by many attendees who were embarrassed by my work, and was insulted by some organizers who told me flat out that they had no idea why I'd even been invited. "We're gay second and fans first, Perry."

Lesson Number Eight: Decide who your real audience is. You will try to expand it, but realize where the expansion should take place. I did have a small group of fans in the science fiction community, but they came for my stories and characters, not for the gimmicks and gizmos that propel so much bad science fiction. I realized later that my real audience came from men and women who understood the deeper emotions I bring to my work—the same feelings that were in my poetry. *Mirage* was about these feelings—and the terrible vulnerability of love itself, something that has pursued me, as it has most people, for most of my life.

Because I took some very old publishing advice (Bump your copyright date up to the next year whenever possible; that way, your book has several more months before it goes stale.) both *Sex-charge* and *Mirage* were eligible for Lambda Literary Award nominations in 1991. It is very unusual for one writer to have two different books in two completely different categories, poetry and science fiction (or at that time, "Gay Men's Science Fiction"), named finalists together. The Lammies always follow the American Booksellers Convention (which has given way to BEA, Book Expo America). It was held in Anaheim, California, that year, and I went to it. At that point the awards were held in a plush hotel banquet room; it was still a dazzling and glamorous affair, with an incredible array of writers dressed in tuxes and evening wear. As my two categories were announced, I closed my eyes and cringed. Neither of my books won, but I was happy simply to be there. A few days later I did a reading at the old A Different Light Bookstore in West Hollywood; this was what I'd really been wanting—to be an openly gay, passionately involved writer; to have something important to say to people, and move them.

Final Life Lesson: Books touch people one at a time, unlike other mass forms of media. There is an intimacy and immediacy to books that is like no other. If I have become a bigger person through my

involvement with writing and publishing, I am very grateful. And if I
have been forced ever to be a smaller one, I genuinely regret it.

FROM *MIRAGE*

Here is a short passage from Mirage. *It describes Albert and Greeland's
"landing" on Earth, where they merge at Jones Beach into the bodies of Wright
and Alan, two lovers from New York.*

Passively, Wright's hand—the fingers cold, like rubber—was
guided to touch Alan's balls. They floated incredibly loose
and warm in a pouch of waving skin. Wright's fingers became
warmer and warmer, until they identified what he was sure was a third
testicle. It was slightly larger than the other two and moved on its own
in Alan's ball sac. Wright felt unexplainably contented; the water no
longer void, cold, and frightening. He couldn't account for the feeling.
He had stopped thinking rationally. He had stopped being Wright for
a moment, then he recognized Alan in a way that was new—foreign to
anything he'd ever known; and finally, ancient and familiar.

He knew, somehow, he'd actually seen Alan like this before.

He encircled his friend's waist and pushed him slightly up, above
him underwater. He buried his face in Alan's groin. The hairs waving
from Alan's crotch tickled his face; he began to suck, carefully, on
Alan's third testicle.

Alan's cock enlarged. Wright massaged the third ball, and then
placed the fattened head of his friend's penis in his mouth. He sucked
Alan all the way, until his lips reached the hilt of the younger man's
cock. Alan, his eyes closed but inwardly opening to another self,
caressed his own third ball, mingling his fingers with Wright's. The
water became warm and golden. It rippled with light. It began to
bubble at that delicate seam of flesh where Alan's penis and scrotum
met, as his syrup, the seed from this new third ball, surged into Wright's
throat.

We lay on the sand for a long time. Wright turned to me and said,
"What's happened?"

I said, "We're here, Greeland."

THREE POEMS FROM *SEX-CHARGE*

THOTH

You have embalmed me
with your beak and cock,
stoking each cache
        with your cracked spice.
How I lie
in your winding sheet, sleeping
        past the wake
of our small end,
a whiter corner in your light,
curled toe to toe
against your parts.
        But still
you shift when you've brought me
to sleep, stitching yourself
quickly in the pocket of my heart.

Even in the earth,
I can feel your stalk,
springing about, locking against my seams.
        Without eyes, I cry
for you to come forth, to slip
out of my mouth and pull me from death.
Like a trick, you take
each organ from its vase
where it waits to be dressed
in my life again;
        and a tongue of me, moistened,
whips to the top,
where I, physical,
hot by your touch,
hang—breathlessly—in the air:
like dust.

Jan. 1977

[Note: Thoth was the Egyptian god of wisdom and writing. In the poem I have expanded him to include death and the forbidden erotically-charged intensity of it. This poem was originally published in *Ganymede*, a small very underground 'zine published in England by Steven Waters, who was pursued by local magistrates for publishing work often seen as pedophilic. Waters was in fact very much into ancient, classical forms of boy worship, and he reprinted work by earlier, mystical gay (or "Uranian") writers like Ralph Chubb.]

TAKE IT SLOW

Take it slow
and burn me up, the way
Horowitz approaches Scarlatti,
his blood barely moving at the finger tips;
the way Magellan met the Indians,
one eye on gold, the other on
annihilation (till a dark hand axed
            his head off
                in the red tides before Bermuda);

take it slow
and let my tongue
roll over your neck,
then down across your collarbone
and further yet, burning
on the belly hairs
like a wick stuck in cognac
fed by the sweat from your gummy navel;
then slip my teeth on your nipples
while they harden and you pinch
at my nuts, ripping from my mouth

like a shark from a boat,
only to return, eager for the danger
to us both: as the end appears
like a silvery crust

before the channel darkens and we grope
for a voltage that stings like a fish,
swacking oxygen between us
pushing open light
pushing open me to you
till finally we fit and your breath
becomes mine in a rush of willing skin,
seamless, delicious, white to my touch
and your lips begin to suck
and lick and go: till all
resistance backflips up,
dissolving, satisfied, to air;

then you, still in my hands, take it slow
all the way down,
down to the hilt;
and the crack, and the nubby, wicked places
where even the hairs don't grow.

March 31, 1986

THERE ISN'T ANY DEATH

There isn't any death
but only constant life
lingering in the cells and the marrow
and the eyes of the world,

and how private
is this vision, this spinning

filament of grasses
and gentle seeds that blow, and birds that fly back
on their way to the sun,

that often we miss the evidence
of turbulence and glow,
of after-peace and still dusks

when the winds seep in
to the joints of rocks and tree trunks,
when the branches

whistle like coyotes
and the clouds skidding through
the distance make remarks

about ages and ages,
and lifetimes that repeat
themselves forever down below.

Jan. 2, 1990
Ridgefield, CT

[Note: Byrne R.S. Fone chose this poem to be the last entry in his
829-page *The Columbia Anthology of Gay Literature*, from Columbia
University Press. He felt that after the AIDS Crisis, this poem gave us
hope—which I believe it does. It was also the last poem in *Sex-charge.*]

Q: Who has most impressed you at a reading and why?

*Easy: Michael Klein. He's wonderful. He and I both understand that a poet has
to do the very heavy lifting, make the huge thing happen, go bigger and deeper
than yourself and find what you are looking for in something other than just your
own limitations.*

SETH
PENNINGTON
&
BRYAN
BORLAND

SIBLING RIVALRY PRESS

SETH PENNINGTON and **BRYAN BORLAND** are the publishers of Sibling Rivalry Press. Based in Alexander, Arkansas, and founded in 2010, its mission, in the words of the incomparable Adrienne Rich, is to publish work that disturbs and enraptures. In its first four years, Sibling Rivalry Press has published a Lambda Literary Award Winner in Gay Poetry, a Pushcart Prize-winning poem, nine American Library Association-honored titles, and one of *Library Journal*'s "Best New Magazines." In addition to *Assaracus*, Sibling Rivalry Press publishes *Jonathan: A Journal of Gay Fiction* and *Adrienne: A Poetry Journal for Queer Women*, plus chapbooks, full-length collections of poetry, anthologies, digital singles, eBooks, and the occasional novel.

THE DESIRE TO SHOW YOU
TO EVERYONE I LOVE

I

A second ice storm—one that kept us
away, one that keeps us on
the anniversary of Pearl Harbor:
a date we forgot until
Sexton served the reminder.
I served myself a glass of water
with a big slice of lemon split
at the line where perception
shifts, looms large: the rind, a flag
of brighter yellow, dotted like some
Seurat piece if he forgot shadow.
Bryan, I decided these rights, these
causes and conversations have been
on repeat too long and at some glacial
pace. Every argument is ninety percent
underwater. The smaller part is caught
enticing me, while I turn insular,
a lemon round, ripe, and know
I have no time for any of this not-you.

II

I have no want for parties or politics tonight,
Sweetheart. You see the waltz of exhaustion
in my eyes, switch on the lights, ask our guests
to leave, declining the invitation to another parade.
You turn down the bed; for this I'm grateful. I know
these walls we build with jagged bones of the absent
leave our seats empty at tables of friends who pay too
much for wine and crowd, who wonder where we are
and when we'll arrive until they forget us forever,
down the rabbit hole, gone. I promise you

> I grieve
> none for this.

III

> I grieve some
> for lack of grief.

On my part—my quiet fits, the attention,
when I bundle it and run past midnight
on a wooden ocean of suburban streets
and lamps that pronounce themselves once
I have passed them. I fear you growing
weary of me when I behave below myself. But
I know that because of me you see above
our house the sky and are amazed each day.
Before, you didn't notice. I did, but found it
no matter until I could show you. Now
when I work a garden it's to show you
how I care. For you alone. And the hope of
a child, five you say. I imagine a farmstead
or a city to grow them and teach what it will,
what each might—as long as we aren't numb;
as long as waters hold us and do not overtake us.

IV

Last night, yes, I dreamed five children, a tribe
and a kitchen where you baked bread. These after-
noons snowed in have such ways of melting
the fingers of logic that run through my hair. There is little
sense of order today; the cat gone missing five months ago
appears fat and happy on the back porch. You worry
I'll tire of you; what to make you believe the absurdity
that I will always be with you? What to make you
understand my fear that you will run when I show
you one too many faces? What to keep you
from leaving and appearing again, belonging
to another, your heart wild as a once feral cat?

V

In sleep
we share whole conversations
only remembered in small truths
like the branding pocked-moon
scar of glass, the infantile
hum of sleep song.

Waking
we hatch in a closeness
double-yolked beyond the intimacy
of my hand, always to come
on your thigh; my tongue to trace
the marble of your ear.

Naked
on the blue beach of bed,
what we are left with
is what charges us:
the power that ranges within us.

VI

Wulf   the mystic tells us not to place weight on herds
of symbols   spit on cave walls   scratches in buffalo
skin that spell our names   says they are everywhere
we look once we learn how to see   in every city we visit
framed in museum   there's us   remember the photograph
of the sisters with our faces   *were we Crow*   the twin eyes
of Chicago brothers   the oldest boy's knuckles bleeding
ink   the letters   *l o v e*   on each of four knuckles   we write
gentle postcards for our future selves to find   frontiers-
men of dusty west   wanderers of northern brick   do you
remember how many times we have failed   we try
again until we get it right   in the easy wild
of these shared sheets   we learn to read
the sky   how the patterns of stars repeat   I follow the curve
of your belly   you touch the freckle on my right ear
we are growing accustomed to this repetition

VII

Who's Afraid of Virginia Woolf? Elizabeth Taylor
keeps yelling at us. It's not a question any more, but it is
a decision to make. We have written the story of our son.
You already wrote the poem, "invented his knees."
I want him, but I cannot decide if selfishly or selflessly;
already I took your hand when I gave you my birthday to
share with our anniversary. My family. My life and baggage.
There's not much more to me. Don't call this false modesty.

VIII

Certain sins can be beautiful. I'm thinking
of greed, this hungry want of you, of every foot of dirt.
I told Gilson how I've allowed myself to become
dependent, how the welding of my needs to your hips goes
against everything I before believed. We're taught
to love only so much until we hold something
back for the inevitable days when the birds fall
from the sky and we bleed from behind. That happens,
I suppose, and who knows how we'll change
by the time it's our decade in these books? The truth is
your dirt does not scare me. I'm better with you
than without, even when it hurts. I want it all. This
is no time for mercy.

IX

I will cut the gold
    strings from my guitar to
    tether your worry.

I will hold its body
    to your mouth when you tell me that history
    is our future; it will sound down your throat.

I will place its back
    along yours and lose the definition:
    what is an *instrument*? what is a *man*?

I will remember, if
    I could sculpt, how your calf would keep
    my fingers wet, my tongue dry.

I will drink you
    like snow, like a milk still steaming with mother.
    I will leave none of you behind.

X

The ice melted; you spend your evenings
in the coffee shop. You pour hot chocolate for
blind boys. I see you behind the counter wearing
my black T, your finger ringed with silver-me. This
will be the last of us here: one job ends, one job begins
(the papers we push to call ourselves poets). Our lives,
I think, will be full of changes like this. I have not come
here often to write—find all my lines rhyme with casual
chatter or your half-burned smile. In the early days,
before you rolled the refrigerator down Kavanaugh
to move from one place to another, these
were our nights. There is a certain magic to the
memories now that I know they'll be just that.
And what are memories but dreams we hold as far
into the morning as we can; unless we etch them
in stone; unless we make them story or prayer
to repeat when your faith or mine needs fire.

XI

I welcome the steady rake
of nostalgia: the two boys
falling in love over poems,
coffee & Cointreau. You're
reading Rich again, that hard
mother that reigned us in
and tore open what we read
as our lives in the pauses
between thoughts. I remember
the light in those stops like
a Quaker might feel. That respect
for being. That acknowledgment
of breathing. I am growing again, slow,
but I wonder when the reverse will hit
and the boy brain will return—

I will settle into a new day job with
the new year; my few debts
will leave then; I will stay.
Question: is this
a fear: a wolf fenced
or is this satisfaction,
what gamble family entices?

XII

You revise a poem in the study. Around the corner
I sit in the orange chair brought from your mother's home
and read *American Poet*, sticky with peach jam from
yesterday's breakfast, Merwin's "The Room" clinging
to "For the Anniversary of My Death." Our dog sleeps
exactly between us, lulled by the usual sounds:
clicking keys, turning pages. If you learn
nothing from me, understand the debts
are never satisfied. They cling to your
fences like honeysuckle. One kindness waters
another which waters another. It never ends.
I cook you dinner tonight; you fry our eggs
in the morning. We find double yolks
for a reason. Fathers or no, we have
what we need: a thousand poets growing
us into men, a thousand poems with
lines like flares above this sea.

KIRBY CONGDON

CYCLE PRESS

KIRBY CONGDON is a poet, essayist, playwright, and artist based in Fire Island Pines and Key West. A contemporary of the Beats, he eschewed their approach to language and became a figure of the underground literary scene of the 1960's. Through his Cycle Press, which he established with partner Ralph Simmons, Jr., and through other ventures, Congdon published and promoted the work of many artists, writers, and poets. An accomplished visual artist, he has exhibited work in solo and group exhibitions since the 1960's. Consistent mediums include metal work, found objects, drawing, and collage.

Q: You are a poet, an artist, a playwright, and a composer. Can you discuss if and how these various strands inform each other?

Surprisingly, different forms of creative work do not seem to relate to each other. I am in one mode or I am not. I think a kind of explanation may be that while I have always wanted to set a poem to music, the rhythm in a poem never fits in very easily for me with the rhythm in a melody. Ira and George Gershwin or Gilbert and Sullivan could do it, but, apparently, I cannot be two people at the same time.

Q: Through your own Cycle Press and other editorial positions, you have become a legendary figure in the independent press. What role has that platform played in disseminating the work of American poets?

I don't feel I have had any effect on the history of poetry. Any recognition is appreciated, but I always wonder, "Is the compliment genuine? Is the writer or speaker sincere or reliable in the big view of things?" I would like to prove that competition does not belong in the arts. It is the work itself that will (or will not) survive for its own sake. There is no accurate judge of it except for the artist's own opinion. That is all he can go by. The rest is mostly just gossip.

Q: Between Key West and Fire Island, you live in two near-mythological locations in terms of gay culture and history. Can you share how this part of your life has influenced your work?

I was not conscious of being gay in particular until I deliberately tried it out. My personality was an introverted one, but, somehow, never negative or depressed. When I did commit myself to who I was more fully, I submitted my work to the very first deliberately gay publication, One, in 1954, and gave up my safe nom de plume (Alden Kirby) after I had used it once. I needed to be me, not an actor. One of these poems in One was later set to music and sung at Carnegie Recital Hall when homosexuality was still a no-no. While all my work is gay poetry simply because its author is gay, I have always tried to avoid convenient categories. Some of my work has been erotic because of my sexual experience but I have not been attracted to the pornographic because, again, that is categorizing taboos as attractions simply because they are socially forbidden. The naughty has never had anything to say beyond spiting its own inhibitions.

Q: What is your view of the small press today?

The small press is the antidote to commercial and academic success. It is where America defines itself and sets its standards. It is out of the spontaneous work of people doing their dedicated best that a civilization can rise.

Interview by Darren Jones
Originally Published by *Salt* (Key West, Florida; Winter-Spring 2013)

THREE POEMS ON THE EMPYREAN

LIBRATION

On the pond's sleeping edge
a tree's reluctant creak rips open afternoons
like a lost cry at night
tearing up the quiet in a private grove
only disturbed by a random breeze.
The sky, stretched taut
between a network of limbs,
lets the ragged noise of leaves slip loose
as though a sorrow's thin blue color,
a universe too much to bear,
was pouring down through a rift in the air.
That universe, self-composed once more,
lies like a dark summer lake;
as pride would stand against complacency
I break the surface of such conceit,
with the toss of a turbulent stone.
Inside concentric circles I hear the echoes
in the punctual plunge of relief
when, generations later, violence breaks a peace.

ON THE BOOK OF JOB

Our experiences are instruments
a body's brain orchestrates
with here a missing note
and there an accent lost
or a lyric goes wrong
in an off-beat song.
Our solo is sung
for its own reward
in grief or praise
from some unknown score
recorded in the timelessness of silence
for a forgotten age or more
while a chorus of stars
celebrates our absence
with constellations on parade
as those eulogies cross an empty sky,
so dark! if our own lights
of rhyme and reason
are passed on by.

FOCUS

What comfort comes looking out
from our stance under cover of the sky?
We have named the lights as that moon,
those stars, exploding here and there,
or the sun with its steady stare
that pagans praised with monuments
to understand how to handle enigmas
with fearful, cautious care
when everywhere the unique
is as ubiquitous as the universal is rare.

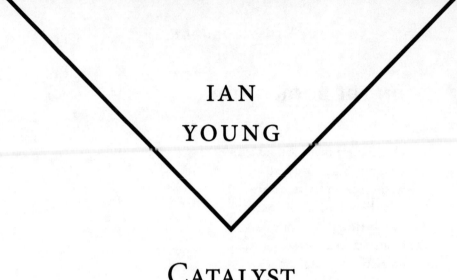

IAN
YOUNG

CATALYST

IAN YOUNG was born in 1945 in London during a severe air raid. He calls it "the night Hitler tried to kill me." Over the years he has been a poet, licensing clerk, editor, microfilm photographer, book reviewer, bibliographer, warehouse manager, small press publisher, dresser for a female impersonator, short story writer, psychohistorian, bookseller, and supervisor of street newsies. He has been active in the Peace, Civil Rights, Gay Liberation, and AIDS Dissident movements, has studied and practiced ceremonial magic, and is an avid stamp collector. At the moment he is writing a group of short stories set in London in the early 1980's; some of these have appeared in *Jonathan* and *Chelsea Station* magazines and in international anthologies. His most recent books are *Encounters with Authors* (Sykes Press) and *Out in Paperback: A Visual History of Gay Pulps* (MLR Press). *The Radical Bishop and Gay Consciousness: The Passion of Mikhail Itkin*, which he edited with Mark A. Sullivan, will be published soon by Autonomedia. He lives in Toronto with Wulf, a props builder, in a house of many books.

Q: What are you currently reading?

I always have a few books on the go. At the moment they are: The Crisis of Global Capitalism: Open Society Endangered *by George Soros;* Last Night at the Viper Room: River Phoenix and the Hollywood He Left Behind *by Gavin Edwards;* Joseph Anton: A Memoir *by Salman Rushdie;* I Will Bear Witness: A Diary of the Nazi Years *by Victor Klemperer;* Faun *by Trebor Healey.*

THE CHANGELING LOVER

I found my secret lover.
He gave me a silver key.
I made him swear a promise
That he'd remember me.

My lover was a changeling.
He fled without design
And played among the sunny fields
And died before his time.

I felled my lover's tombstone
And dug for him there
And wrenched his body from the earth,
Into rain and air.

And as I took him in my arms,
Who was so blond and clear,
He turned into a clutch of bones
And soil that smelled of fear.

All skull he was and tatters,
With eyes that did not see,
Who uttered, crumbling in my hands,
"JUST YOU REMEMBER ME!"

THINGS AS THEY SEEM

In dark spring rain
on a chilly shore
I found a shell
from the ocean floor

I held it
stillness all about
it was your distant voice
I heard call out

In summer rain
in the empty air
there was no-one, no-one
yet I saw you there

running, running
toward me again
on a chilly shore
in fine spring rain

The fallen leaves
piled red by the hedge
the clothes you dropped
by our window ledge

The empty hall
the cup by the stair
in the slanting sun
and empty air

A ticking fire
and skittering mice
in the roof for warmth
in a world of ice

Was it your footsteps
coming near
through halls of deepening snow
at the end of the year

Wherever I watch
or listen or dream
your absence troubles
things as they seem

THE KNIGHTS
from the Russian of Yevgeny Yevtushenko

Like Nature, they remain unaltered,
capable of no new hate or passion,
making their sacrifices without inward change.
Encrusted in the cold glitter of their mail,
the fear glints from the cracks where courage shone;
their old success no longer understands
and sees no good in understanding.
Clustered in ranks they ride;
the tatters of their giant horses
flap on the wind.
Obsessions drive them like a plague
toward their fate.
They are not changed from what they were.
Yet how they are subject now,
prone to decay,
afraid of the real, afraid of battle.

IAN YOUNG

MEMOIRS OF A PUBLIC SPEAKER

Once upon a time it was me.
I was the lost man,
the empty man
at the corner of the eye,
the Scribe, something occult in the offing, not
Orthodox.

Coping with me gave them something to do.

They despaired of me. For them, my gestures
were a ritual for hands,
a clatch of secret signs,
and what I said
only gave grounds for hope.

I gave thoughts wings, made things
speak in a thing language, un-
natural.

Where I walked
I burned the wet grass and it sizzled.
When I talked
children closed their eyes and listened
and fell off cliffs.
The words of my spells made my tongue taste of words.

When I stood, the horizon
twisted behind me.
All the clocks ran backwards when I slept
and when I woke, alarms
rang inside hearts.

My pen was a single cloven hoof
leaving a black track, my book
was a curse.

Where I looked
the air glistened and shook.

My eyes were dense
circles of blank knowledge. A blink
meant "come and get me," a wink
"who knows?"

My tricks
worked but not always
fast enough, yet even as they took me,
wands fell from my sleeves,
pentacles snuggled in my hand.
My agents I'd never seen were abroad in the land.

The dark lasted a while—
I had not been long at ease.
Shut off from speaking,
confined to my own syllables,
Heretic, Magus,
Poet-Witch, I burn
in my own time,
in my own language.

AUTUMN WOODS AFTER BOOKHUNTING

It's a good day for me
when I find a gift to send you—
the right book,
found in a trance,
as though the Guide
got through just a little better than usual
for a few moments.

Do you know
those old poems, I wonder—
by Tu Fu, Wang Wei and the rest?
The poet sits outside his mountain house
among the fir trees,
writing a poem
with a delicate brush—
a poem about how he misses his friend
who has gone to a faraway place.
The poet,
no longer young, imagines
he and his friend will be reunited
when they have grown old
and have long grey beards.

The air is chill now
as I walk through the woods.
The leaves are falling
and the days are getting shorter.
Kneeling to run my hands
through the red and yellow leaves,
I remember the first time
I ran my hands through your hair,
your lips on mine.
Your magic touch.

IAN YOUNG

REFLECTIONS OF A CATALYST:
RUNNING A SMALL PRESS IN THE SEVENTIES

"Catalyst: a substance that initiates or accelerates a chemical reaction . . .
something that causes an important event" - Princeton *WordNet*

One sunny summer day in the late 1960's, I was sitting quietly at a big table in a spare basement room with eight or ten "editorial committee" members of something called *Catalyst*, a competent, rather dull literary magazine produced by graduate students at the University of Toronto. I and my friend and fellow poet Michael Higgins, both newcomers, were the non-academics of the group.

Above ground, birds were singing and hippies were playing slow-motion Frisbee on the lawn, but in our editorial offices, which bore a depressing resemblance to Hitler's bunker in its last days, we were aware only of the interminable droning of our "Lady Chairman" (there were no chairpersons in those innocent times). She was holding forth on her favourite theme, the pressing need for a writers' lounge. She had been thinking out loud on this and other subjects for at least half an hour—a performance made no easier to endure by an unfortunate facial tic which jerked her features into a momentary convulsive rictus about every sixty seconds.

As she drifted into another of her pet subjects—the many and subtle connotations of the word "catalyst," I caught the rolling eye of the only one of my academic colleagues I felt friendly enough to have a coffee with, a burly British ex-paratrooper called John Holland. Clearly, he was in silent torment. When our leader ran out of things to say about "catalyst" and returned to the need for "a clean, bright place where readers as well as poets can come sit and enjoy themselves," I interrupted, suggesting that this sounded like the sunroom of a good lunatic asylum.

Holland's Pan-like features brightened into a machine-gun burst of chuckling. The ever-silent Higgins blushed. Everyone else looked nervous. Our Chairman's parents donated much of the operating capital for the magazine and this was why everyone was so patient with her. I had violated an unspoken rule; clearly, things could never be the same. It was the end of an era—and more to the point, the end of term, with some committee members shifting their attention to exams and others preparing to abandon *Catalyst* and the halls of academe altogether. The bunker was ripe for a coup. By autumn, we three Englishmen had taken over. Our pensive Chairman and the others moved on, and so did the philanthropic parents.

Our British triumvirate published one more issue of the magazine before my two colleagues dropped out. I might have done the same if the Gay Liberation movement hadn't come along. It was long overdue as far as I was concerned; I had tried to get a gay group off the ground a few years before while I was helping a friend run a weekend campus coffee house, but few gays or lesbians, on campus or off, dared to come out publicly. Then, inspired by the Stonewall riots in 1969, the first Gay Liberation group in Canada was formed, just in time to coincide with a nationalistic outbreak of Canadian literary publishing. The time seemed right to transform *Catalyst* from an unremarkable, college-based journal into a publishing house specializing in books and chapbooks of new gay poetry and fiction. I had very little money and virtually no publishing experience.

Over the next ten years I published thirty titles by Canadian, U.S., and British writers. Apart from a short period working in an art college in England, I earned my living as a freelance writer based in Toronto and New York. As freelancing provides a precarious and meagre income for all but a few, there was never much money for me or for the press. Fortunately, my habit of amassing and selling unusual book collections paid some of the bills. I learned how to economize and acted as my own staff—everything from editor and chief designer to parcel wrapper and traveling salesman.

My main criticisms of many of the existing small presses were that too often their products looked unnecessarily shoddy and unattractive, and that little real effort was made to distribute them. I wanted to publish attractive-looking books at low prices and to get them into the hands of readers starved for good gay writing. I wasn't interested in commercial books but in literary writing that wouldn't be published unless I did it.

When I began, big houses often excised anything suggestive of homosexuality, and even small, noncommercial presses were less receptive to gay writing than they are now. The gay presses that later began sprouting up had not yet been seeded. House of Anansi, one of the most adventurous of the new Canadian publishers, had issued my own *Year of the Quiet Sun* in 1969, but its co-director, Dennis Lee, was exceptional. A few years before, his Muddy York Press had published (with help from Margaret Atwood) Edward Lacey's first collection of poems, *The Forms of Loss*, the first openly gay book to be printed in Canada. Lacey, born in Lindsay in 1937, had been expelled from the University of Toronto, for reasons which remained obscure: one graduate student told me Lacey had entered their dining hall wearing a piece of sod on his head (a relatively minor transgression, it seemed to me). After three years of psychiatric care, he had suddenly vanished, perhaps into the interior of South America. I wondered about him.

The first Catalyst titles were by young Toronto writers (gay, straight, bisexual; ultimately, I was concerned more with the quality and freshness of the work than the purported sexuality of the authors). Richard Phelan and Wayne McNeill were high school students when Catalyst released their first books. Michael Higgins, a North of England lad, was an habitué of Yorkville, Toronto's briefly popular hippy haven. Graham Jackson was an aspiring playwright when Catalyst published his stylish, bitter-sweet stories and his *Dance As Dance*, the first book of dance criticism in Canada. (I quickly learned that in the minuscule province that is dance criticism, to give notice of a colleague is merely to encourage a rival. There were few reviews.)

The roster of unknown Canadians included the B.C. writer Judith Crewe whose *The Ancient and Other Poems* came unsolicited in the mail. There were two American poets on the list, with very different styles. The dour observer of urban mores, George Whitmore was later to become a member of New York's Violet Quill coterie which also included Edmund White and Andrew Holleran. The most romantic of classicists, Thomas Meyer was the long-time amanuensis of the Jargon Society, Jonathan Williams' North Carolina literary press, renowned for its fine design and dogged promotion of such diverse poets as Lorine Niedecker, James Broughton, and Alfred Starr Hamilton. (Jargon Society had published Irving Layton's breakthrough book *A Red Carpet for the Sun* and two other Layton titles in the 1950's.) There was also a duo of seasoned English men-of-letters, Kenneth Hopkins (born 1914) and Oswell Blakeston (born 1907).

Kenneth Hopkins had been the friend and semi-official biographer of the Powys brothers. A chronicler of the Poets Laureate, he had made his living as a freelance writer for many years, publishing mystery stories and sundry commissioned volumes including one in which he took a particular perverse pride, a pseudonymous quickie biography of Liberace. In an early letter to me, Kenneth described himself as "a woman lover, rather glum than gay (though with many gay friends)." He was certainly an enthusiastic lady-fancier but when planning to visit Toronto, he asked if I could suggest "a very cheap motel or rooming house within striking distance of you and in a good run-down redlight district full of pink youths. . . ." The book Catalyst published, *The Dead Slave,* a clever pastiche of Martial, reflected Kenneth's occasional appreciation of the boys, as well as his ability to imitate just about anyone's poetic style. Kenneth took teaching jobs where he could get them, and we were able to meet on the banks of the Rideau during one of his summer stays at Carleton University. He had a number of Canadian interests and through his own small press, Warren House, published a volume of poems by the venerable Jacob Jehosaphat Mountain, the Norfolk-born versifier who became the first Anglican Bishop of Quebec.

Oswell Blakeston was an equally prolific author with over a hundred books to his credit on subjects that included Edwardian glamour cooking, zookeepers, the island of Heligoland, and cats with jobs. He received his invitation to publish with Catalyst by bending over on the street outside his house. As he came out of his door one morning he saw a letter on the sidewalk "right where the dear little postman had dropped it" and picked it up. It was addressed to him—a message from me asking to publish his novella *Pass the Poison Separately.* This could easily have been an incident from one of Oswell's own elliptical writings. The book got very good reviews, one of which hailed "this talented young Canadian author." He had been a well-known writer in Britain for decades.

A favourite drinking companion of Dylan Thomas, Oswell had been a pioneer of British avant-garde films, had cruised the streets with Eisenstein, and been propositioned—on a different evening—by Aleister Crowley. His many volumes of innovative fiction and poetry included *Hop Thief* (1959), the first novel with an index, and *The Cat with the Moustache* (1935), the first popular book to discuss hallucinogenic drugs. Oswell was also a painter, exhibiting in butcher shops and prestigious Finnish galleries. His partner, the painter Max

Chapman, had been a protégé of Oscar Wilde's artist friends Charles Ricketts and Charles Shannon.

I was determined that Catalyst books would be attractive as well as inexpensive, and enlisted a varied roster of artists, including the highly respected Illinois designer A. Doyle Moore; Wilton David, an eccentric, transsexual illustrator from Louisiana; New York street activist Ralph Hall whose drawings were influenced by the psychedelic art of the Sixties; and a young Toronto student, Lennel Goodwin. With them on board, we even won some prizes for design.

In the early 70's I began seeking out and collecting books and chapbooks by the new generation of poets who were enthusiastically casting off the old taboos against queer content. These I reviewed regularly in The Ivory Tunnel, a column I contributed to the Toronto-based newsmagazine The Body Politic. My growing chapbook collection fed my novice publishing projects and, by 1973, I was able to edit an anthology of the best of the Stonewall generation, alongside older out-of-the-closet writers like Tennessee Williams, Thom Gunn, Kirby Congdon, and Christopher Isherwood. The Male Muse was published by John and Elaine Gill's Crossing Press in Trumansburg, New York, publishers of the binational magazine New American & Canadian Poetry.

By 1974, I was spending much of my time in New York City, and in the fall of that year, I walked into Penn Station and spied a slim, dark, long-haired boy standing on a large cabin trunk and gazing around the station like a lost waif. It was Gavin Dillard, and this was our first meeting. I had wanted to publish his poems as soon as I'd read them that summer while visiting Jonathan Williams and Tom Meyer in Yorkshire. Jonathan told me they'd been written by a boy from his own hometown, Asheville, North Carolina, and showed me some strange photographic self-portraits the teenage author had sent. I wrote to Gavin asking for more of his writing. When it came, I offered to publish a small book as soon as I got back to New York City. Gavin wrote back from Asheville asking if he could come to New York and work on the book with me. So, here I was, helping this hippyish prodigy lug his worldly belongings into a cab and up the stairs to Craig Kennedy's second floor flat on St. Marks Place over the Gem Spa—not a health club but a magazine shop that stocked anarchist newspapers. We lived there together while working on Twenty Nineteen Poems and a second book, Rosie Emissions. Gavin later moved to California where he became an escort to the famous and closeted, eventually publishing a delicious, tell-all memoir, *In the Flesh*.

Our first days in New York coincided with the middle of winter; typically for New York the building's boiler had broken down, and Gavin and I had to manipulate huge bowls of steaming water from the kitchen stove to pour into a bath. We could have bought an electric fire, but published *Twenty Nineteen Poems* instead. I remember our crunching through the snow (Gavin wearing novelist Wallace Hamilton's overcoat, some few sizes too big; me in my regulation-issue leather bike jacket) and stopping to peer into the window of an East Village gift shop, trying to go in but finding the women inside too wary to unlock the door, convinced that two such dubious-looking characters were intent on robbing them.

Anyone who has tried to sell books—or anything—door to door has to be able to shrug off rejection. Bookshop personnel have an endless list of reasons why they won't stock the particular goods you're offering. If your wares are saddle-stitched productions, though store managers don't actually hiss "*Spineless!*" they nonetheless claim they have no way to display them. Or they drawl, affecting an air of disdain, "Poetry doesn't sell!" When confronted with this line, it is futile to point out that the book you're offering is a collection of short stories. With booksellers, as with publishers, the ostensible reasons don't mean a thing; only the refusal—or the acceptance—is real.

Merely being a small press with no distributor is often enough in itself for a refusal—"too much paperwork." Or: "Oh, you're from Canada? We had a Canadian book here once. Didn't sell." And of course, the all too frequent resistance, in those days, to anything gay. I remember taking Gavin's *Rosie Emissions* to the now defunct Small Press Book Center just off Christopher Street. The cover of the book featured the comely author naked to the hips. "Frontal nudity!" they gasped. "We couldn't possibly put that on our shelves." I pointed out that two-piece bathing costumes for gents had long gone out of style. No sale. Another well-known store cheerily ordered a dozen copies of Tom Meyer's *Uranian Roses*, only to refuse delivery of them later. And of course, the big publishers always got paid first, with little left over for anyone else.

Even in the few gay bookshops, one's wares had to conform to certain sometimes annoying standards. Gay's the Word in London,

England, would carry nothing overtly Christian. Manhattan's Oscar Wilde Memorial Bookshop was careful to stock no volume containing the word "nigger." Owner Craig Rodwell was roused to indignation whenever he encountered this word (or any of his other proscribed terms) and all books were scrutinized for offensive verbiage, regardless of context. James Baldwin's works were among those that seldom made it past the censorship stage. But Rodwell liked me because I had been, like him, a gay activist before Stonewall, and because I never lectured him on how he should display my books in his shop. (For me, getting them actually onto store shelves was triumph enough.)

Not all my tribulations came from booksellers. Equally exasperating were the printers who put books together with pages in the wrong order and the writers who posted unsolicited manuscripts (often of *major* length) while neglecting to enclose return postage—or, almost as bad, sent U.S. stamps to my Canadian mailing address. They were politely informed that as the United States had lost the War of 1812, Canada remained a separate country; their U.S. stamps had been forwarded to American prisoners.

One day I received an unexpected phone call. "This is Ed Lacey," said a voice like dry paper about to ignite. The mystery man of Canadian letters was making a brief stopover in Toronto before returning to South America as English tutor to the former President of Brazil. Lacey apparently had a new manuscript—the distillation of twenty years of poems, many of them with gay themes and Latin American or North African settings. He had been planning to publish them himself, he said—the book had even been sent to the printers— but had decided distribution would be too much for him to handle. His friend John Robert Colombo had suggested I might be able to help. "I'll publish it!" I blurted into the phone. "You haven't seen it yet!" Lacey reminded me.

We met in a room in my parents' basement that served as Catalyst's warehouse. Like William Burroughs, Lacey had a dry humour but seldom smiled. Thin, and oddly pale for a world traveller, he never seemed to quite relax. Leaning forward in his chair, he alternated between listening intently and fidgeting with the typescripts he had brought with him. It was difficult to tell whether he was intrigued by our conversation or anxious to excuse himself and drift out the door. "I do not consider myself a poet by profession," he told me, "Poetry is a sort of by-product of my life. . . . Insomnia has always been my muse."

Edward never stayed in Canada long enough to overcome his mental picture of the country as the frigid, joyless wasteland he had experienced in the 1950's, and he soon fled once again for parts unknown, having agreed that Catalyst would take over distribution duties from his own (stillborn) Ahasuerus Press. *Path of Snow* thus became the first of his two Catalyst books. They are Canadian (and gay) classics, though still little-known, largely because of the author's self-effacing nature and the fact that he preferred cheap hotels in Lima to literary soirées in New York.

I was constantly trying to get grants and perks for Catalyst's writers. At one point, during one of my stays in England, the possibility of British publication for some of them was suggested by Brian Atkinson, a English literary agent I came to refer to as Mr. Mutual. I was skeptical of success but willing to lend an ear. When we met in a London pub, Brian turned out to be a married man of sixty plus, randy as a goat, and with something of a one-track mind. The English prospects of Catalyst authors soon evaporated in a beery haze as Brian, making a necessary run for the lavatory stalls, laid a couple of meaty hands on my forearms and attempted to drag me in there with him. "Come on in for a bit of mutual!" he whispered with a chummy leer. "Mutual" was Brian's familiar term for what the English call "helping a friend out," my erstwhile agent's preferred form of sexual activity. As it happened, he had no luck, either with me or with finding publishers for Catalyst's authors. Full marks for trying though.

Then there were the two Henrys. Literary publishing, being utterly noncommercial, tends to rely on subsidies of one sort or another, but benefactors are few. The two Henrys were two separate potential patrons in the city of New York who shared a first name and an interest in gay writing of the hotter sort. The first was Henry Geldzahler, New York City's Commissioner of Cultural Affairs and a much-publicized friend of art and artists. He had a particular liking for the erotic poems of Dennis Cooper, whose first full-length poetry manuscript, *Idols,* I was then trying to finance. Henry G. invited me to visit him at his offices, and I was hoping that he might at least put me on the track of some funding for Dennis's book. As it happened, he looked at me in a slightly frightened way, listened to my remarks about Catalyst, cast a glance at the books I had brought for him, and literally ran from the room, claiming a pressing appointment with the mayor. Dashing past me, he tossed me a twenty dollar bill (worth more then of course) as though throwing a bone to a dog, gasping "Send me some books!" I left the samples I had brought on his table. Later I told my fellow poetry publisher Jonathan Williams what had happened. "Well," said the voice of experience, "I've known Henry for twenty years and that's twenty dollars more than I've ever gotten out of him." *Idols* was eventually published by Felice Picano's Sea Horse Press, with Catalyst as the Canadian co-publisher.

The second Henry was Henry Sofejko, a rich socialite who spent most of his money on the pursuit of venery. One night he showed up, rather tipsy, at a bookstore poetry reading accompanied by a handsome, expensively dressed youth. After the proceedings, he invited me to join him and his young friend at the piano bar of the elegant Carlyle Hotel. He indicated a handsome cheque would be forthcoming for future Catalyst endeavours.

After causing a scene with the majordomo, Henry S. led our little party to a centrally-placed table and proceeded to regale nearby patrons with an anecdote about how he had just picked "Julian" up on the street. As Henry held forth excitedly, I turned to make small talk with his boyfriend. "Julian," it turned out, was not his real name and Henry had apparently spun the same pointless story on previous occasions. Doug, a.k.a. Julian soon began to tell me about the play he was writing. This seemed to infuriate the now sulking Henry, who scowled at me and flew into a rage. "What are you saying to him?" he demanded, as though we had been plotting his overthrow, which might not have been such a bad idea. As the hotel pianist gamely tried to make himself heard and the other patrons started grabbing their furs and slipping away in groups, I realized that whatever reason Henry had for inviting me into his evening, no cheque, handsome or otherwise, would be forthcoming. I excused myself as politely as I could. As I stood up, Henry, now thoroughly inebriated, convulsed himself in a burst of indignation, spilling my glass of Coca-Cola all over his exquisitely tailored lap. I bid goodbye to Julian/Doug, who I guess was used to such scenes, and rejoined my poet friends scarfing down the last of the sandwiches and pickled onions back at the bookshop.

Alas, Catalyst attracted few "patrons." The Ontario Arts Council provided some much appreciated funds. And somehow, we managed to survive for over ten years. While in 1970 it had been the only gay press in existence, a few years later there were several, including Winston Leyland's Gay Sunshine in San Francisco and Felice Picano's Sea Horse in New York. I closed Catalyst at the end of 1980 simply because I ran out of money. A one-man, vest-pocket-and-kitchen-table operation, it could not have survived without the efforts of many—including its printers, particularly Tim and Elke Inkster of The Porcupine's Quill, who produced the most handsome of our books.

And there were unexpected perks. Once or twice, Catalyst was able to recommend a few writers for small grants. The journalist Tim Guest was one of them. A raven-haired radical who wrote a "gay youth" column, Tim was said to be "the most beautiful boy in Toronto." He invited me over to check out his grant purchases—a mattress and a pair of cowboy boots.

The Stonewall rebellion and the coincident revolution in Canadian publishing were both high energy movements that emerged, relatively healthy, from the turbulent decade of the 1960's. Their joint influence led to my unprecedented little 1970's venture, which as it turned out was the first of many. By the time we ceased operations in 1980, my friend Doug Wilson's Stubblejumper Press in Saskatoon was ready to take over, publishing novelist Peter McGehee's first book and the first gay and lesbian guide to Canada. And I left for England, just in time to attend the launch party for London's newest publishing house, Gay Men's Press.

IAN YOUNG

MAKING *THE MALE MUSE*

"The gay revolution began as a literary revolution."
- Christopher Bram, Eminent Outlaws

In 1972, I decided what the world needed was an anthology of gay poetry. Three years earlier, the unprecedented events at the Stonewall Inn in Greenwich Village had galvanized the North American gay community, and it didn't take long for the shock waves to reach Toronto. I had played a part in starting Canada's own gay liberation movement, and had turned my small literary magazine, Catalyst, into the world's first gay publishing house. Now the first gay liberation magazines had begun to spring up—*Gay, Come Out, Come Together, Gay Liberator, Fag Rag, Gay Sunshine, The Body Politic,* and others—and their small ads often included notices of self-published and small press chapbooks by an emerging cohort of gay poets. I sent for them all.

These kitchen table publications were among the first out-of-the-closet, unmediated communications of the Stonewall generation, and the best of them were impressive in content and/or design. But their distribution was limited to local reading venues, mail order sales, and a few friendly bookshops. And in an environment where gays were still largely invisible, people were starved for information, images, and literature. I felt a well-edited anthology showcasing the best of the new, openly gay poets—alongside the few older, established poets who had dared to disregard the taboo against openly gay writing—would have broad appeal to a growing number of contemporary readers.

There had been a number of earlier crypto-homo anthologies of course, but none of clearly designated, openly gay poetry. A covert, anonymously edited compendium, *Men and Boys,* had been privately circulated in the 1920's. Whitman disciple Edward Carpenter's *Ioläus* (1902) and Canadian poet Patrick Anderson's *Eros* (1961), both billed as "anthologies of (male) friendship," were lightly disguised historical miscellanies. My book would take gay poetry all the way out of the closet. Maybe—just maybe—I could interest an established publishing house.

I set about contacting every good gay poet I could find, as well as putting out a general call. My efforts soon paid off. *The Male*

Muse: A Gay Anthology was published in 1973 by John and Elaine Gill's Crossing Press. One of the more professional and substantial of the smaller presses, Crossing Press was based in Trumansburg in upstate New York, the same town where Robert Moog had set up his first synthesizer factory. The book, featuring forty poets from five countries, sold very well, becoming a "small press best seller." A decade later, a follow-up collection, *Son of the Male Muse* introduced a second group of prodigiously gifted poets.

My anthologies, I decided, would include only living writers. And I wanted to mix poets of the new, Stonewall generation with others already established. This would show a historical continuity, and the presence of well-known names would (I hoped) give the book weight and help it on its way. Robert Duncan had come out in print as early as 1944 with his boldly pioneering article "The Homosexual in Society" in Dwight Macdonald's magazine *Politics*. Allen Ginsberg of course would be essential. Edward Field was another early out-of-the-closet gay writer, and an influential one, with his revolutionary pop culture poems. Paul Goodman, Harold Norse, Robert Peters, John Wieners, and Jonathan Williams were just about the only other openly gay American poets from older generations. More problematic would be a number of writers who were known to be gay but had not quite come out or were playing peek-a-boo. These included W.H. Auden, Tennessee Williams, and Thom Gunn. I would write to them anyway, and hope for the best.

Of the British, I wanted to include the prolific James Kirkup, Oswell Blakeston, master of the brief poem, and John Lehmann, memoirist, editor, publisher, and all around man of letters; all three were personal favorites. My friend Timothy d'Arch Smith suggested adding Brian Hill, who became the oldest poet in the book, born in 1896. And Canadian expatriate Edward Lacey was a must; his early book, *The Forms of Loss,* had been Canada's first openly gay collection.

Among younger poets, I had a handful of names from the U.S. and Canada and one each from Ireland and Australia. Ads and notices in gay magazines brought a few more to my attention. On this basis, I began to write to the various poets or their representatives.

Looking back, one can oversimplify by dividing the contributors into a few handy categories. First, the bohemian pioneers of gay poetry from earlier generations: Allen Ginsberg readily agreed to let me have anything I wanted free of charge; Edward Field, John Wieners, and Harold Norse were also key, as were Blakeston, an avant-garde artist in fiction, painting, and film as well as poetry, and Kirkup, world traveller and collector of dolls and perfumes.

Second, a diverse group we might call the gentlemen poets—more conservative in personal style than the bohemians, including three poet/publishers, Jonathan Williams, John Gill, and John Lehmann. I had found some of Jonathan's elegantly wry poems in E.V. Griffith's *In Homage to Priapus*, a literary miscellany published in 1970 by Greenleaf, a porno house. Several of my contributors had appeared in this collection, which was something of a breakthrough in combining pulp and literary authors, poetry and fiction.

There were unclassifiable loners like Kirby Congdon (sometimes bracketed with the Beats but never really one of them), Edward Lacey—peripatetic, alcoholic, depressive, with a quietly resigned, unsentimental view of the world, and Paul Goodman, novelist and anarchist social critic, who died suddenly while the book was in progress. I took the liberty of dedicating *The Male Muse* to Goodman as he—a married man with a family—had stuck his neck out when very few dared.

Among the more reluctant who had to be coaxed were Tennessee Williams and Thom Gunn, both of whom soon came all the way out of the closet. During my one meeting with Tennessee, he was amiable but vague and possibly drunk or stoned. I used his deliciously intriguing "The Interior of the Pocket" which I eventually chose over my own favourite "My Little One." Gunn claimed that "gay poetry, like political poetry, is something I can't do well." I disagreed of course and he relented, allowing me to use "The Feel of Hands" and "Blackie the Electric Rembrandt" (about tattooing), though not "The Beaters" which he described as "a poor poem." There was also the utterly heterosexual and not at all reluctant Michael Higgins, with "The Boy Botticelli Painted."

Other younger members of the tribe included Jim Eggeling from Texas, several Canadians—including two from the quiet college town of Guelph, Ontario, not hitherto known as a hotbed of sodomy— and a strong San Francisco contingent including Ronald Johnson, Paul Mariah, James Mitchell, Edward Mycue, Michael Ratcliffe, and Richard Tagett. From Ireland there were Jim Chapson and James

Liddy, who provided the book's title ("I am flattered to be invited to invocations of the Male Muse. . . . Bless him!")

There were also specific poems I was determined to include. Perry Brass's "I Have This Vision of Madness," one of the most powerfully moving gay lib poems, Robert Duncan's "Sonnet I: Now there is a love of which Dante does not speak unkindly . . .", and Christopher Isherwood's campy, to-the-point "On His Queerness," of which he wrote "since it's for the Cause, I don't want any fee." And I had to include "The Night Is Wild" by the late, previously unpublished, Jay Socin, whom I excepted from the "no dead poets" rule.

Poets were included in alphabetical order to mix up different styles and younger and older contributors. There were highly sexual pieces like Edward Field's "The Moving Man" and Jimi Kirkup's equally sensual "The Drain" ("Those three young workmen have had it up again . . ."), poems about movies and prison and gay couples, leather poems by Congdon, Paul Mariah, and Ralph Pomeroy, and the crisp, vivid romanticism of Hill (who apologized to me for not being "modern") and Lehmann.

Of course, some poets demurred, notably W.H. Auden, who sent an explanatory note: "My answer is, I'm afraid, no. When I write a poem for publication—naughty limericks to amuse friends are another matter—I always try to write it in such a way that it makes sense for any reader, whatever his or her sexual tastes." And I would have liked to use Jimmy Centola's dramatic monologues "Change for a Dying Queen" and "The Divas of Sheridan Square" but for reasons which I'm ashamed to say I've forgotten, they ended up not being included. Perhaps we were simply unable to contact him.

The Male Muse was published in 1973 and was very well received. (Although when the book was imported into Britain, the shipments were seized by Her Majesty's Customs and some books were destroyed. Legal action had to be taken to prevent further interference.) It went through five printings and two editions, hardcover and paperback. A new gay literary scene was fast emerging. I was particularly pleased to hear that a new magazine devoted solely to gay men's poetry, to be called *Mouth of the Dragon*, would begin publishing in New York in May, 1974.

In the summer of 1973, I made my first trip to New York City from my home in Toronto. The main reason for my trip was not literature but magic: I had been invited to be the guest of the Trinidadian theosophist Michael Gomes, a correspondent of the legendary Israel Regardie. Dr. Regardie, psychotherapist and former secretary, for a time, of Aleister Crowley, was the man who had revealed to the world the occult secrets of the Hermetic Order of the Golden Dawn, as originally conjured up back in 1887. I was eager to make contact with practitioners of Golden Dawn rituals and the Gomes/Regardie connection seemed the best way to go about it. As it happened, my visit to Mr. Gomes was aborted and my quest for the G.D. took another five years. But as I was in Manhattan anyway, I decided to look up some of the *Male Muse* contributors—and the editor and publisher of the proposed new poetry magazine, one Andrew Bifrost.

Andy Bifrost was originally Alan Morris. He had left his former job as a stockbroker and, with the support of a patron, Prof. William Kinter of Baltimore, had decided to slough off his old identity, change his name, and serve the cause of gay poetry. I phoned him and we arranged to meet at his home on Cornelia Street in Greenwich Village. When I arrived, the budding publisher was standing in the street, having misplaced the key to his apartment. Andy Bifrost was a wiry man of medium height, with an enormous head, a shock of long, tangled hair, moist, prominent eyes, and a splendid Roman nose. I quickly found myself hanging out of a window several stories up, holding onto his ankles while he shinnied alarmingly across two planks above an ancient air shaft. Though this was rather an odd introduction to New York life, I somehow knew that Manhattan was where I wanted to be. The secrets of the Golden Dawn would have to be postponed, just for a while.

The years 1969 to 1981 were the unprecedented Gay Lib decade, with an extraordinary flowering of gay art, literature, and theater. Emerging gay poets now had places to publish! I kept track of them, contacted those I considered the most interesting, and began collecting the material that would become *Son of the Male Muse*, published (also by Crossing Press) ten years after the original volume. In that intervening decade, attitudes—of both readers and writers—underwent significant changes. Thom Gunn, asked in an interview whether the Gay Movement had helped him as a poet, said: "Yes, very much I think. In my early books I was in the closet. I was discreet in an Audenish way. If a poem referred to a lover, I always used 'you'. I figured it didn't matter, it didn't affect the poetry. But it did. Later I came out, and Ian Young included me in his *Male Muse* anthology, so that I'd officially gone public. Now, I wouldn't have expected it to make so much difference as it did. In the title poem of *Jack Straw's Castle* I end up in bed with a man, and I wrote this quite naturally, without a second thought. Ten years ago, I doubt if the incident would have appeared in the poem. It wouldn't have occurred to me to end in that way."

I made a decision that no one who had been in the first anthology would be included in the sequel; contributors to *Son of the Male Muse* would be, for the most part, poets whose work had come to public attention (or at least, to my own attention) since the earlier book. There were contributions from thirty-nine more poets, among them Steve Abbott, Antler, bill bissett, Richard George-Murray, Thomas Meyer, Felice Picano, David Emerson Smith, and Jack Veasey. I was especially pleased to be able to include several writers whom I met and was able to encourage before they were published, or as they were just beginning to publish—Wayne McNeill, Dennis Cooper, Daniel Diamond, Gavin Dillard, and Tim Dlugos.

By the beginning of the 1980's, Felice Picano, a good editor as well as a good writer, had founded Sea Horse in New York, and in my birthplace of London, England, I attended the launch party of Gay Men's Press, founded by the able trio of Aubrey Walter, David Fernbach, and Richard Dipple. I was accompanied by *Son Of . . .* contributor Jamie Perry, the accomplished Golden Dawn magician (though still a teenager) into whose orbit I had been drawn two years before. The gay lit scene was really getting going. But of course, everything was about to change drastically. We were in for a shock.

In the years to come, over a dozen contributors, including Jamie, would die in the AIDS epidemic, many of them later included in Philip Clark and David Groff's 2009 anthology *Persistent Voices*. Andy Bifrost and Richard Dipple were also AIDS casualties. A second *Male Muse* sequel, *Return of the Male Muse,* which I edited together with Gavin Dillard, never found a publisher. But as poet William Bory put it, "the Muse doesn't fool around for too long." In spite of severe losses and trying times, several excellent anthologies did appear, including Gavin's *A Day for a Lay: A Century of Gay Poetry* (1999) and John Barton and Billeh Nickerson's *Seminal: The Anthology of Canada's Gay*

Male Poets (2007). And by 2010, Sibling Rivalry Press had taken up the torch to become an exciting new publisher of LGBT poetry and fiction. The Male Muse was in as good shape as ever.

"Nor are we barren, as our detractors claim," Gavin Dillard wrote, "for we have ceaselessly given birth to the muses of tomorrow."

SUBMIT TO *ASSARACUS*

We encourage submissions to *Assaracus* by gay male poets of any age regardless of background, education, or level of publication experience. For more information, visit us online. [siblingrivalrypress.com]

SUBSCRIBE TO *ASSARACUS*

Visit our website to subscribe to *Assaracus*. Your subscription buys you four book-length (120+ pages), perfect-bound issues of our grand stage for gay contemporary poetry. Our standard subscription prices are $50.00 for one year/United States; $80.00 for one year/ international. Inspired by the long-running journal *Sinister Wisdom*, we are also proud to offer a special hardship subscription price of $20.00, which includes four issues of *Assaracus* shipped anywhere in the world. We ask that you pay full price should you have the ability to do so, but one's degree of good fortune should never impede access to poetry. Likewise, we will provide free copies of *Assaracus* to LGBTIQ support groups, mental health facilities, and correctional facilities by request. To request a free copy or subscription, please email us. We also offer the option of voluntary "sustaining subscriptions" for various dollar amounts should you wish to financially contribute to the longevity of *Assaracus*. Such support will also help us to continue offering discounted and free issues of the journal to those who might benefit. [siblingrivalrypress.com]

WHAT WE'RE READING

Bryan: *Leaflets* by Adrienne Rich

Seth: *Moon-Whales and Other Moon Poems* by Ted Hughes

CPSIA information can be obtained at www.ICGtesting.com
Printed in the USA
LVOW12s0401270314

379088LV00001B/3/P